Leadership, Perspective, and Restructuring for Total Quality

Leadership, Perspective, and Restructuring for Total Quality

An Essential Instrument to Improve Market Share and Productivity
by Eminent Leaders of America's Most Competitive Companies

Richard J. Pierce, Editor

ASQC Quality Press
Milwaukee, Wisconsin

Leadership, Perspective, and Restructuring for Total Quality

Richard J. Pierce

658.409
L4342

Library of Congress Cataloging-in-Publication Data

Leadership, perspective, and restructuring for total quality : an
    essential instrument to improve market share and productivity / by
    eminent leaders of America's most competitive companies : Richard J.
    Pierce, editor.

    p.   cm.
   Includes index.
   ISBN 0–87369–101–5
   1. Total quality management   2. Leadership.   I. Pierce, Richard J.,
HD62.15.L43   1991   91–9659
858.4′082—dc20   CIP

10987654321

ISBN 0-87389-101-5

Acquisitions Editor: Jeanine L. Lau
Production Editor: Tammy Griffin
Set in Baskerville by Carlisle Communications.
Cover design by Wayne Dober.
Printed and bound by Port City Press.

Printed in the United States of America

 ASQC Quality Press
310 West Wisconsin Avenue
Milwaukee, Wisconsin 53203

Contributors

Robert L. Loughhead
Chairman, President, and CEO (Ret.)
Weirton Steel Corporation

Forrest E. Behm
President, International Operations (Ret.)
Corning Glass Works

William W. Eggleston
Corporate Vice President, Quality (Ret.)
IBM Corporation

Richard J. Pierce
Group Executive for Quality Operations (Ret.)
General Electric Corporation

Colin W. Williams
President and CEO (Ret.)
Aspen Institute for Humanistic Studies

Contents

Preface

This book is designed for leaders and managers who seek to establish Total Quality at their companies. The intent is to bring together leaders who have successfully applied approaches to Total Quality with the leaders and managers who seek approaches. The book is appropriate for leaders and managers at all levels, in all types and sizes of companies. They must all be involved in the quest for Total Quality.

Total Quality efforts are underway in many leading American companies. Increased productivity, improved competitive position, and greater market share are major goals. Total Quality is essential for competing in national and international markets. However, progress is restrained as there is need for better perspective about the broader meaning of Total Quality, its new place in business, the management philosophies upon which Total Quality is based, and the magnitude of the changes for which there must be commitment and implementation.

The authors maintain that leadership by the Chief Executive Officer is paramount, since only the CEO has the power to commit to and implement the extensive changes required. They hold strong beliefs that a foundation must be built that addresses the restraints being encountered by leaders and managers.

A leader must create an effective and enduring quality foundation. This involves changing attitudes and management style throughout the organization and adopting the philosophies that underlie Total Quality. Perspective is gained through the heritage from past philosophers, business leaders and statesmen who employed capitalism to create the greatest national economy the world has ever known. Also, it is useful to learn the philosophies and approaches used by Presidents and CEOs who have established a foundation for Total Quality tailored to their individual companies. Further, it involves learning the reasons for America's decline and how foreign competitors overtook us. This leads to focusing on a few but vital advantages foreign companies have structured that Americans must match. The foundation also includes the creation of short and long-term missions and objectives, along with values, all key considerations in the quest for Total Quality.

With a solid foundation established, a leader needs guidance for planning and implementing the many other changes essential to establishing Total Quality. Four of the co-authors hold appointments as members of the Board of Examiners of the Malcolm Baldrige National Quality Award. They believe that the guidelines for the Malcolm Baldrige Program fit well within the broader framework needed to achieve Total Quality. They also believe that the Malcolm Baldrige National Award helps to define Total Quality.

This book is for the thinking leader who wishes to develop a strategic quality plan but first needs to establish a foundation for Total Quality.

Often leaders do not give sufficient attention to the larger framework of guidelines for establishing a quality foundation. They may proceed too soon, to assigning management teams to fulfill the seven primary criteria of the Malcolm Baldrige guidelines. This approach achieves temporary euphoria within the company, followed eventually by loss of credibility by employees, disenchantment by managers and cancellation and return to square one by the CEO.

This book is intended to broaden the perspective of the leader and to stimulate the leader's thinking to select and apply the approaches best suited to the company. Continuity is achieved with broad criteria for building a foundation with help from the Malcolm Baldrige guidelines.

In PART ONE, Robert Loughhead provides perspective about the philosophies that are the basis for Total Quality. He gives guidance for establishing a foundation and he explains what Total Quality is and the essential changes that must be made to achieve it.

In PARTS TWO, THREE, and FOUR, Forest Behm, William Eggleston, and Richard Pierce draw on their experiences at their respective companies to provide their philosophies and approaches for establishing foundations and fulfilling criteria for Total Quality.

In PART FIVE, Colin Williams improves the perspectives of leaders with articles from a heritage of past philosophers, business leaders, and statesmen who employed capitalism to create the world's greatest national economy.

In PART SIX, Richard Pierce informs what the Malcolm Baldrige program is about, where it fits, and some effective approaches for its use.

In the APPENDIX there are articles by Presidents and CEOs who have installed their foundations and individual versions of Total Quality tailored to their companies, by internationally recognized experts, by an eminent Japanese professor who has practiced both in Japan and the United States, and the Department of Commerce's Associate Director for the Malcolm Baldrige National Quality Award.

Perspective: What Total Quality Is and What Changes Must Be Made to Achieve It

1

Robert L. Loughhead

Chairman, President, and CEO (Ret.)

Weirton Steel Corporation

INTRODUCTION

Robert Loughhead provides perspective for, and stimulates thinking by, the official seeking an excellent approach for establishing Total Quality. He informs us that most of the commitments the official must make require restructuring to be effective.

Loughhead presents guidelines for putting into place a foundation that is crucial to achieving effective and enduring Total Quality. These guidelines involve:

- Enlarged Meaning of Total Quality
- Attitudes
- Management Philosophies
- Leadership of People
- Communication and Environment for Listening
- Short- and, Particularly, Long-Range Missions
- Company Values and Ethics

Also, Loughhead presents guidelines about the scope and magnitude of essential changes that must be made to install Total Quality.

These guidelines provide continuity for the book. The authors that follow pick up on these guidelines and supplement them with their philosophies and the changes they have applied at their respective companies.

1

Restructuring for Total Quality 1

The subject of management philosophy has been promoted in nearly every way possible in the past decade. Quality, the *sine quo non* of excellence, has also been a favored topic of books, articles, lectures, and seminars in recent years. Corporate restructuring, largely financially oriented, has often been in the forefront of the business world in this decade.

There are many reasons for corporate restructuring—some of them valid and some not. We have all seen examples of both kinds. Many of the goals to be sought through restructuring are just as vital as financial considerations. One of these goals is the pursuit of quality.

Quality is now recognized as essential for improved productivity, increased competitiveness, and enhanced market penetration. While there is a broad consensus as to the need for quality, the understanding of what quality is and what must be done to achieve it are points not yet universally accepted.

If Total Quality, that is to say quality performance, is to be achieved, it must be recognized that "quality" is much broader than simply meeting the specifications, physical requirements, or performance capabilities of a particular product.

While quality performance is the responsibility of everyone in the business organization, it must begin with and be led by the chief executive officer. He must lead the revolution to achieve Total Quality. He must develop the concept of quality as a management philosophy and provide a design for improved quality performance.

Current prescriptions for management excellence typically refer to a "new enlightenment." Managers are rightly advised to become obsessed with quality, to pursue lower costs relentlessly, to stay close to customers, to develop a deep involvement with employees and a virtual partnership with suppliers—all in the quest for excellence. These are prescriptions needed to achieve the healthy state of Total Quality.

3

It has been said that the best definition of quality might simply be conformance to customers' requirements. Certainly meeting customers' requirements is a vital ingredient in achieving Total Quality that might best be described as leadership.

It is instructive to consider where some of the current emphasis on excellence and quality have come from. Are these approaches the result of the evolution of management theory, the development of strategic planning, and the science of goal setting? Or are they, more accurately, a return to some of the fundamentals that preceded the science (art?) of strategic planning upon which successful businesses have always been built through cooperation among workers, managers, suppliers, customers, and bankers? These questions are worth considering in the pursuit of Total Quality.

Quality is not achieved through any magical fixes, regardless of whether such efforts are technical or psychological. It is achieved through people—most particularly through leadership of people. This leadership must come from the chief executive officer.

One of the things that leadership embodies is taking the right approach at the right time. Leadership is a dynamic art, not a static science. It requires meeting the challenges at hand and those in the foreseeable future, not dwelling on nor being bound by the past.

Examples of leadership as an art can be seen in a number of notable cases in American business history in which chief executive officers virtually created strategic business plans on a corporate level and led their companies to outstanding success. Now some of those same corporations are led by a "new breed" of CEOs who have achieved excellence in their own right. More often than not, in the course of that achievement these CEOs have nearly eliminated large corporate planning departments, pushed planning down to division or business unit levels, and acquired reputations as hip shooters rather than contemplative analysts and planners as their predecessors had been known. The earlier generation CEO was often the product of management theory; the new person in charge is the product of straitened economic reality. To be sure, each suited the needs of the company at the time; each also pursued "excellence" long before the term became the buzzword it is today.

In short, the true (and truly legendary) business success stories— tales of excellence—are those of CEOs employing approaches that work best to solve the problems at hand and ahead, problems with quality, people, customers, suppliers, costs, and competitiveness. Management theory and changing economic reality are radically intertwined in this history of American business excellence: successful managing is fundamentally a dynamic exercise.

As is the case with any plan to bring about change—to restructure and to achieve total quality—it is important to look first at what went wrong. If the CEO is to become the agent of change, and indeed must if change is to happen, it is worthwhile to examine how American business got to the place where it now finds itself, with the focus on quality.

For many years American manufactured products were quality leaders throughout the world. "Made in U.S.A." was virtually a stamp of approval—assurance of high quality. Why, then, have American manufactured products lost their worldwide quality dominance? There is no single answer to that question. It is, however, widely accepted that other nations' manufactured products in many cases are superior to products produced in America.

In seeking answers to America's lost dominance as a quality producer, I believe some rather interesting questions can be raised—such as:

- Has the quality of American manufactured products declined in absolute terms, or has it declined only relatively to the product quality of other nations?

- Did American quality stay about the same while other nations' quality got better? or

- Did American quality actually improve while other nations' quality improved even more?

- Did America's quality slip because its technological development lagged that of other nations?

- Did America's "cost to produce" rise so high relative to that of other nations so as to cause American producers to "build-in" less quality, thinking (rightly or wrongly) that costs could thus be lowered?

- Did American management's lack of aggressiveness toward export markets cause it to wear blinders to the idea of rising quality levels as a global competitive issue?

- Did the adversarial nature of American labor-management relations cause a lessening of the quality of American manufactured products?

- Did management pressures to produce high volume and the existence of production-based incentive systems lead to a deterioration of quality in the American work place?

- Did American management, workers, and consumers drift into the ideological trap that "perfection is impossible" and a certain level of defects is acceptable?

- Was the development of high quality products in other nations and their export to America inevitable, given the postwar rebuilding and modernization in those countries and America's failure to enforce its trade laws?

- Did American management simply fail to recognize, for many years, the importance of quality in improving productivity and competitiveness?

These are questions that CEOs in pursuit of total quality must raise with respect to their companies. And if, as will inevitably be the case, the answers to many of the queries by the CEOs are yes, the restructuring required to bring about total quality in their companies will be of Herculean proportions.

If the CEO finds that the company is lacking in technology, is a high cost producer, has little knowledge of export markets and quality levels required in those markets, has adversarial labor-management relations (particularly at the front line and middle management levels), has production policies that emphasize quantity over quality and pays workers accordingly, and has a culture that accepts a certain "defect rate," then the CEO will also realize that achievement of Total Quality will require great change.

I stated earlier that quality is much broader than simply meeting the specifications, physical requirements, or performance capabilities of a product. Total Quality then, is broader still. It means achieving quality in everything an organization does. It means doing the right things right (the wrong things can also be done right) all of the time. It often means changing the way an organization does almost everything—a monumental mission to say the least.

Not surprisingly, this kind of change can come only from leadership at the top—from the CEO.

The first barrier toward making Total Quality happen is actually the CEO. The first one to change must be the CEO. If he or she attempts to delegate the initial effort, it won't work. Despite the expected outcries from the CEO, such as "my time schedule won't allow my personal involvement in the pursuit of quality," "we have people whose responsibility it is to do that," or "my other responsibilities are more vital to the success of the company"—the CEO must personally lead the charge or it will fail. Moreover, CEOs often should do more of what they delegate and delegate more of what they do.

The CEO must send out a clear message that Total Quality is established as a management philosophy—Total Quality as a way to work and manage. The philosophy must call for quality performance—not just quality control, and productivity improvement—not just product improvement, and improved market penetration—not just market studies.

The key to bringing about the kind of organizational change to achieve Total Quality is commitment. Lest that seem an oversimplification, consider the Japanese example. The evidence seems clear that the single most important underlying force in Japan's becoming a worldwide leader in quality was commitment. Obviously they employed the right tools—quality circles, statistical process control, just-in-time inventories, and others. Those things are all important, to be sure, but they are just tools for executing a plan of commitment. After World War II, Japan, as a nation, decided that if it was ever again to achieve respectability in the world, it would have to do it with superior quality products. Japan made a commitment to achieve that respectability by taking the necessary steps.

That same kind of commitment must be made by CEOs before sending out the message on the pursuit of Total Quality. They must decide that they are going to do it. Making the commitment is the first thing the quality control manager has to say to the CEO.

As set forth in later chapters, there are various specifics to the CEO's fulfilling the commitment, and commitments are required from many other constituencies as well. In most cases, those commitments can be met only by organizational change.

Looking back over my own years as a CEO, I see that the single most important thing that I have been trying to effect is change—change in attitudes, change in relationships, change in the approach to the people side of the business, and often changes in my own views. Attitudes toward quality, people, costs, productivity, customers, and suppliers should never remain simply fixed.

Rosabeth Moss Kanter, author of the best selling book, *The Change-masters,* says, "Before improving quality or changing the culture or business direction, people at every level must understand and buy into the vision."

That is so true. One of the commitments that the CEO must make is that the quest for Total Quality will involve all of the people in the organization—not just management. If the CEO really means to meet the commitment, he or she must see to it that the employee involvement process is established throughout the company. At the very least, CEOs must personally demonstrate a working knowledge of the process and certainly they must meet periodically with leaders and facilitators. It must become clear to everyone in the company that this is what the CEO wants and intends to see happen.

The first step toward establishing the employee involvement process is recognition of the fact that a vast storehouse of knowledge exists in the minds of workers and managers who have been doing their jobs for many years, often not in the way they believe the job should be done, but in the way they have been told it must be done. In essence, management's move toward employee involvement amounts to management's recognition of the importance of the person.

Although not widely practiced in a meaningful way, employee involvement is becoming more widely espoused for a number of reasons. A major reason is that management continues to look for new solutions to the old problems of:

- How to overcome alienation in the work place
- How to combat static productivity
- How to raise morale
- How to instill trust and dignity
- How to generate cooperation and improve relationships
- How to change attitudes
- How to replace fear with fairness

Total Quality can never be achieved without lasting solutions to these problems.

The CEO must direct the organizational change to accommodate the employee involvement process. In so many ways, quality depends on people, so it logically follows that nearly everything that affects people can affect quality. A culture change is needed.

Often the CEO has to direct the change from a workplace culture that calls for "finding out who did something wrong and meting out swift punishment," to an environment that provides for "finding out why something went wrong and fixing the entire system." That fixing may deal with people, materials, or machines. If the organization does not change to the latter approach, one thing can be assured—whatever went wrong will go wrong again and Total Quality will remain elusive. That kind of organizational change does not come easily—changing attitudes never does.

As the CEOs cause the employee involvement process to become a part of the organizational change, they must do so with the understanding that it is intended to do much more than make everyone feel better about recognition, participation, and implementation of ideas. CEOs must reach agreement with the leaders of the process that goals such as improved productivity, better quality, and lower costs are on everyone's agenda. It must not be allowed to become merely a social gathering where workers and managers reflect on how nice and cooperative they are—such a system may be goodness, but it is not necessarily good.

The CEOs must hold themselves up to be the champions and leaders of the band where Total Quality is concerned. They must make it clear that "we are going to do things differently around here and we are going to do them right—in production, in sales, in human resources, in finance, in administration, in purchasing, and in every part of the business."

Unions or other representatives of the work force must commit to the processes of employee involvement, statistical process control, communications, and other quality performance efforts and, to the greatest extent possible, keep them separate from ordinary labor relations matters. This commitment is vital.

With respect to labor involvement in the pursuit of Total Quality, the human side of the equation cannot be overlooked. In his article, "A Labor Perspective on Participative Management," Howard Samuel, president of the AFL-CIO, Industrial Union Department, stated, "QWL means Quality of Work Life, and QWL programs are supposed to improve the quality of work life as well as productivity and quality. Too often the emphasis is entirely on the latter, while the former is forgotten." This message is important to all who would embark upon the road to Total Quality.

Worker representatives, be they union or otherwise, must agree to fill such roles as quality team leaders and members, steering committee members, co-directors with management, and spokespersons for quality performance—performance, not quality control. They must develop ownership of the plan with management to achieve Total Quality. These are new roles for individuals. They will fill them if they are convinced that the top executive means to change the way the company operates and is serious when saying quality comes first.

The CEO must demonstrate his or her seriousness by leading the effort to get employees involved. The CEO must also provide resources and training to develop employee involvement and must convince people that it is not just one more program or fad, but rather something that is to become a basic process in the daily operation and management of the business. Establishing a climate for listening before the employee involvement process can be undertaken is also a necessary task for the CEO.

The climate for listening must be established for effective communications to begin. And effective communications and employee involvement are absolute prerequisites for the achievement of Total Quality. Total Quality will be achieved only if all constituencies—the

CEO, top management, middle management, front-line supervision, the work force, and union officials—are all well informed and involved at the outset and remain committed.

Given the proper commitment from the CEO, executive and middle management must also bring commitments to the table if Total Quality is to be achieved. Key executives must become the medium for the message—an extension of the CEO's office in the quest for Total Quality. The CEO's quality goals must become their action plans. While one might expect top executives to handle this role quite readily, experience teaches us otherwise. Key executives may have been accustomed to coming to the CEO with various plans and objectives developed from the bottom up. The pursuit of Total Quality, since it starts at the top, may in a sense turn their organization upside down. It is, however, a matter of leadership. The key executives must represent an extension of the CEO's leadership—not as agents of control, but as agents of change. Unfortunately, that role may not come as easily to key executives as one would hope.

Brian L. Joiner and Peter R. Sholtes, in the article, "The Quality Manager's New Job," maintain that there are serious problems with management by control and a better alternative is Total Quality leadership. Most conventionally organized quality control departments are not so oriented. Organizational change is required here as well.

Given the right approach by the CEO and proper leadership support from executive management, if there is a critical point at which the effort toward quality performance can go awry, it is at the middle management level. Tom Peters and Nancy Austin, in their book, *Passion For Excellence,* said ". . . quality, above all, is about care, passion, consistency, eyeball contact and gut reaction—quality is not a technique, no matter how good."

If one were to try to define the elements of the leadership role of middle management in achieving Total Quality, it would be difficult to improve upon that—care, people, passion, consistency, eyeball contact and gut reaction—powerful stuff—but perfectly suited to the middle management leadership role. If the CEO can get the quality managers to put all of that in their mission statement, the quest for Total Quality is off to a good start.

Middle management must recognize the critical nature of its role and realize that quite often failed efforts toward achieving Total Quality can be laid at its feet. Middle management must learn to share information with lower ranks and recognize that some sharing of authority is necessary in order to develop a participatory environment, without which Total Quality will never exist. Middle management must also see its importance as a role model to front-line supervision and to the work force in the effort toward quality performance.

And what about front-line supervision? In an article entitled, "Re-conceptualizing Quality," C. Phillip Alexander said, "The answers lie not in the system and methodologies, but in people." That is true, but front-line supervision must change in order for Total Quality to be workable.

Certain specific changes must occur on the part of front-line supervision. And those changes will come only through proper training, designed to convince front-line supervision to change. An important inducement for that change is that front-line supervision must become convinced that the organization is going to change.

Front-line supervision must begin to lead rather than drive the persons they direct. They must become more participatory and less authoritarian. Part of this change requires that front-line supervision begin to implement workers' ideas, wherever possible, without reference to higher authority. Their leadership must become evident if quality performance is expected of the work force.

A major change is required in labor-management relations to support front-line supervision's changing role. Union leaders and workers must begin to recognize the difference between driving and leading and offer their dedication to a "good day's work" so that supervision can abandon its role of police and enforcer, and get on with its role of leadership and participation. This idea represents a major change in work place environment.

I would offer an important caveat at this point. Just as unions must not hold quality performance efforts hostage in labor relations disputes, middle and upper management must not sacrifice good labor relations practices and policies at the altar of quality performance. Any gain will be short-lived and front-line supervision will have been betrayed.

Not surprisingly, the largest constituency of all, the work force, must also make commitments to change if Total Quality is to be achieved.

Perhaps the hardest sell of all is convincing the work force at the outset that improved quality performance on their part, while vital, may bring no added compensation ("what is in it for me"), but that in the long run, productivity and quality improvement are necessary for survival. Understanding of this concept comes slowly because companies die hard—it takes a lot to kill them.

If organizational change is achieved in the form of a commitment to Total Quality, from the top down, workers will respond favorably. Most workers want to produce a quality product efficiently and at competitive costs. There are any number of reasons why they may not be able to do so, but it is management's responsibility to change the organization so that those reasons disappear. Companies that have achieved Total Quality have succeeded in changing the organization.

Training programs for the work force must provide clear evidence that such practices as rigid work rules, strict job classifications, and strident turf-guarding will deter efforts toward Total Quality. The reorganized work place that brings better communications, employee involvement, and responsiveness to ideas, while improving relationships, must also see the removal of these barriers. The effort must be a two-way street. Companies that are on the way to Total Quality are dealing with these barriers.

A very sensitive point in the Total Quality effort has to do with compensation. A strong attempt should be made to tie some part of hourly and salary compensation to quality performance levels and the economic health of the business. That approach recognizes that quality may often be people sensitive and not always system dependent.

In an article entitled, "A Values Oriented Approach To Quality," Ross J. Gilbert said, "Quality is often discussed only in technical terms, such as the application of control charts, or the newest processing equipment. Soft issues, such as communications, interdepartmental relations, and employee attitude are much less prominent." In reorganizing a company to achieve Total Quality, that upside-down emphasis has to be changed.

When pressing for changes in attitude and commitments from the work force, the CEO is likely to hear from the human resources people such things as, "It is very difficult to obtain any broad commitments from the work force as they will act primarily as individuals." Such a dynamic exists to a degree, but the American work force is grossly underestimated. The work force is more intelligent than given credit for, is more interested in quality than most managements realize, has vastly more knowledge about how work should be performed than has ever been taken advantage of, and cares more about the business than management has ever taken time or thought to realize. By and large, the work place is a reflection of and reacts to, what management has been doing over the years. If management changes the organization in ways that I have mentioned, the greatest untapped resource for the achievement of Total Quality is the work force. Instilling trust and dignity in that work place must be a key element in the reorganized environment.

Although many of the current quality experts disagree about how to approach quality improvement, they seem to agree on certain major points. They all recognize that there are no short cuts to quality performance and that the improvement process is never ending, requiring the full support and commitment of individual workers, whole departments, and above all top management. They speak virtually with one voice about the need for change and reorganization of the work place.

There are many detailed specifics in the plan to achieve Total Quality such as quality policies, goals, measurement systems, quality teams, statistical process control, and more. Most of these are covered elsewhere in this text. As mentioned earlier, however, they are tools for implementation—just that and nothing more. Before the tools can be used, before the plans can be implemented, indeed before the journey to Total Quality can begin, everyone in the business needs to learn to listen. Learning to listen brings the ideas to the surface.

Earlier I defined Total Quality as leadership—a short definition to be sure. If forced to flesh it out, I would add that it means getting a personal commitment from, and a realization by, everyone in the business that the customers are king and we are all pledged to give them exactly what they need—defect-free products, that we all have to learn to listen to each other, that the cost of not having quality means the life of the business, and that because quality performance is a process of continuous improvement, change must be viewed as a dynamic process rather than a one-time quick fix. And only through leadership can these things occur.

Quality is also a matter of ethics. Can management expect quality performance on the shop floor if there is a lack of integrity at the top levels of management? And isn't giving customers exactly what they asked for a matter of integrity? Companies have a moral obligation to live up to the promises they have made in advertisements, product brochures, and annual reports. Ultimately, quality performance is the only route to credibility for a company.

Essential Changes: To Build a Foundation and Fulfill Total Quality Criterion

2

To say that change is required in order to achieve Total Quality is an understatement at best. Changes are required in attitudes, in communications, in employee involvement, and in the roles of unions.

It has been said that quality is an attitude. While the two are hardly synonymous, attitudes do affect quality performance. This is particularly true of the attitudes of the workers on the shop floor. Today's shop floor workers' attitudes are different from those of an earlier time. The problem lies not so much in the fact that today's workers' attitudes are different, but rather that management has failed to recognize the reasons for it.

Today's workers are better educated and more mobile than their predecessors. They are not particularly awed by authority, and they want to be more a part of the decision-making process. Today's workers have different priorities and more outside interests. Their jobs may not be the most important thing in their lives.

Many years ago workers' attitudes may have been primarily affected by how well or how poorly they were paid. Now workers' attitudes are affected more by how they are treated, how they are trained, and the general work place environment.

Because of the effect of attitudes on productivity and quality, clearly they must be dealt with in the quest for Total Quality. Change is required. There has been a deterioration of attitudes in the work place and it is important to examine management's role in that deterioration. Too often management has tended to drive rather than lead people. And attitude has usually been treated as a discipline problem rather than recognizing valid emotional, economic, and other reasons for the deterioration. Approaching attitude problems as a disciplinary matter obviously misses the mark. Among the factors that have brought about poor attitudes are worries over job security, unsafe working conditions, authoritarian work place environments, inadequate training, declining standards of living, and an inability to be heard.

Given the fact that the power to make change happen is often largely vested in management, if a different tune is to be played in changing attitudes, management must lead the band.

Improved communications must play a vital role in planning for Total Quality. Merely inundating people with information does not ensure effective communications. Communications must be a two-way affair. Communication systems must provide a means to determine if the audience really believes it is being communicated with, whether the right information is being sent out, whether all constituencies have input, whether there is feedback, and whether the entire climate is conducive to listening and free exchange.

In seeking to establish effective communications, management would do well to worry less about confidentiality and become more concerned with always telling the truth and removing barriers rather than trying to communicate around them. True credibility is rarely achieved in communications without personal involvement by top management, responding openly to questions from those persons with whom it is trying to communicate. The only sure-fire way of determining communications effectiveness is personal, face-to-face meetings and creating an openness in those meetings—again a climate for listening.

Top management must give a higher priority to communications than is normally seen. It is questionable whether the excuse of time constraints is really valid. If top management's time allows for visits to customers, bankers, security analysts, and the media, why not more time for visits with employees? Are any of those constituencies more important than the employees? Or is the dearth of time spent with employees by top management due to the fact that such meetings are often unpleasant, demanding, confrontational, and require answers to hard questions? If indeed they are of that nature, the need for them is all the greater.

When CEOs say in their annual reports that employees are their greatest assets, do they really mean it—do the employees believe it? The gap is very wide between the CEO who speaks of employees' importance in the annual report and the worker on the shop floor. It is difficult to understand why CEOs allow the gap to exist since their principal concerns and those of the workers are common concerns—the survival and success of the business.

It is totally unrealistic to expect that a state of Total Quality can ever exist if employees who must make it happen are not part of an effective communications system.

A number of pitfalls will likely be encountered in establishing effective communications, and they must be managed rather than ignored. Previous failed attempts at communicating may have damaged management credibility, unions and managers may be placed in new and uncomfortable roles, initial efforts may be viewed with mistrust—an effort to get more out of employees, ordinary channels of communication must often be violated by top management in order to gain credibility, and communications efforts may have to compete with other demands for scarce resources.

Employee involvement and communication are essential elements of the plan to achieve Total Quality. Significant change must take place in order to create the kind of environment where employee involvement can flourish.

While it seems obvious that persons who have been doing jobs for many years would have a great deal of knowledge about how those jobs should be done, the question is, why hasn't that knowledge been put to use? The answers are that people have not been asked or if asked, have not been listened to; workers often feel that they are not trusted and in turn do not trust management; and workers do not believe that their ideas will be accepted and implemented, so they remain silent—a credibility problem.

Critics have claimed that the great American Success Story—the American Dream was achieved without employee involvement. Perhaps it was, but the more important point is whether American business has fully utilized all of its resources, including the ideas of its people. It seems that it has not.

Regardless of what has gone before, the world has changed and management must make a major commitment to change the work environment to keep pace. One wonders if some of the major problems that have plagued industry for decades could have been resolved long ago if employee involvement had become a way of life.

There are a number of reasons why the CEO is in the best position to lead the effort toward employee involvement. CEOs are in the best position to commit a company to change. They can provide resources, set the best example at the top—create a role model, and do certain things at the outset by fiat, which may be necessary to get the ball rolling.

Given a commitment at the top to get underway with employee involvement, labor and management have expectations from the process that require attention. All have a right to expect that the process will develop a means of working together and create an environment where interests are common and not alien and where singleness of purpose exists. Employee involvement does not mean employee control. Control is rarely what labor expects. All constituencies must plan for and expect the effort to move from a program at the outset to a process. This effort must become thoroughly integrated into the man-ufacturing process—become a way of life.

Initial management concerns about getting underway with em-ployee involvement often revolve around how to create the desire on the part of the people to become involved. To a large extent, this is an unwarranted concern. Rarely is there any need to create a desire for involvement by the work force. They are eager for involvement. It is simply a matter of properly channeling that desire through training in problem solving, group decision making, and reaching consensus, and then recognizing everyone's right to be heard, no matter what the topic.

Creating interest is more difficult where middle and lower man-agement are concerned. Management must become convinced that it is a better way to manage and that there are tangible benefits. They must be shown that their jobs eventually become easier with employee in-volvement and that quality and productivity can be improved by the process. They must know that it can reduce their costs rather than tax their budgets.

Although not particularly complicated, the process of developing effective employee involvement does contain a few key considerations. In most cases it means change.

The work place atmosphere must be changed to one of trust, respect, dignity, concern, and receptivity. The CEO must set that tone. People must quickly see tangible evidence of implementation of sug-gestions made. Credibility must be established. The philosophy of in-dividuals doing things for the overall good of a group must be instilled. The process must not be allowed to be regarded as a fad, but rather as something that is forever, in good times and bad.

There is a need to overcome the detachment from the work force by management and boards of directors. All constituencies must come to realize that goals and objectives for long range strategies will not be achieved without support from all of the people who have to make it happen. Such support will not come without the opportunity for input. Management must convince everyone that it really believes people matter most. Management and boards of directors must begin to re-alize that strategic planning sessions and board meetings are not the real world. That is a delusion. The real world is in plants (yours, your customers', and your suppliers'), in sales offices, and out where a sales-man is in front of a purchasing agent trying to get an order.

Unions play a vital role in employee involvement. Not all unions have yet decided just what their official positions are on the process. Unions' concerns about employee involvement have to do largely with their suspicions that all the emphasis will be placed on productivity and quality with no regard for the quality of work life. Abuses of the process have created fears in the minds of union leaders that it is a management ploy to get more work for the same amount of pay.

Unions' fears and suspicions of employee involvement can be allayed by providing proper training and by developing sound programs to educate workers about the economic side of the business. The more they learn about how the business works, the more willing they are to become involved.

A current trend in manufacturing operations is to abandon the assembly line, single function, routine approach, in favor of natural work teams. Participation (involvement) and flexibility are inherent in the team approach and fully compatible with the employee involvement process.

Much of manufacturing's present lack of flexibility descends from Frederick Taylor, who some 85 years ago espoused dividing work into discrete, repetitive tasks in the interest of simplicity. One result of this has been narrow job classifications and rigid work rules. The natural team concept calls for workers to perform various tasks instead of one. It has proven to be less boring and more motivational. It has also provided more involvement in the decision making process. Management must surrender some degree of control for the natural team concept to work. Companies that have done this have seen improved productivity. The NUMMI plant in California is an example.

The philosophies of the quality of work life and changing the work place environment are supported by employee involvement. Natural work teams may become an important change to pave the way for the process.

There are some outstanding examples of change that have occurred in recent years, built on involvement and by people working together.

During the past several years, deregulation has been very much at the forefront of the business and political scene. Murray Weidenbaum, President Reagan's original economic advisor, has made some interesting observations about it. He said, "It has been bipartisan; it has demonstrated the power of ideas brought forth and developed by economists, political scientists, and legal scholars to overwhelm entrenched economical and political interests." The process appears to be a powerful achievement. It seems something that could not be done by dictate, fiat, or executive order was accomplished by participation and involvement by all concerned.

The new Proctor & Gamble marketing strategy is an interesting development illustrating change. The company seems to have changed its entire product management and marketing strategy from a single, powerful product manager, responsible for manufacturing, marketing, and all else that related to a particular product, to a team concept involving participation and consensus.

Ford Motor Company is an industry leader in quality. Its chairman has said that the task of improving quality becomes one of gaining the trust of workers. That is a very strong example of change brought about, at least in part, by employee involvement.

Change does not come easily where labor management relations are concerned. However, if workers are given the opportunity to become part of the decision-making process, and if they are accorded respect and dignity and given an opportunity to learn the economic side of the business, changes in technology and new approaches to raise productivity and quality levels will meet much less resistance. These things won't happen at the bargaining table. They will happen by finding ways for workers to become involved. They must happen if a state of Total Quality is to be achieved.

Approach for Effecting Change   3

In order for commitments to be established and kept, it is vital that specific actions be taken by all who will be involved in the quest for Total Quality. Only through committing to and implementing these actions can Total Quality become a process—a way of managing.

Actions are first required of the chief executive officer. The CEO must send out a clear message that Total Quality is established as a company wide goal—Total Quality as a way to work and manage. It must be clear that the goals are not just quality control, but rather quality performance, and not just product improvement but productivity improvement as well.

The CEO must make the commitment that the company is going to achieve Total Quality in everything it does, even if that means changing the way it does everything.

The top executives must commit to provide effective training with a means built in to monitor application in the work place of what has been learned in the classroom. They must give assurance that funds will be budgeted for training and quality efforts in good times and bad. The CEO must establish a company-wide practice (practice—not policy) that a required portion of managers' time will be devoted to training—either receiving training or giving training. Managers' effectiveness in training others should become a part of the performance evaluation system.

The CEO must make a commitment to establish a company-wide communications program and must become personally involved in the communications process. People must be trained to communicate by every means possible. Personal meetings with the CEO (groups and one-on-one), in-house television, telephone hot lines, in-house newspapers, and meaningful correspondence from the CEO are examples.

Assurance must be given by the CEO that managers at all levels will respond, to provide two-way communications. To follow up, the

CEO must personally find out if people really believe that communications are effective once the process is established.

Assurance from the CEO that the quest for Total Quality will involve all the people in the company must be given in the form of his or her commitment to establish the employee involvement process throughout the company.

The CEOs must promise to inject themselves personally into the employee involvement process by demonstrating a knowledge of it, meeting with leaders and facilitators, and speaking at appropriate meetings of teams, steering committees, and facilitators. They must also provide the requisite training resources regardless of the current business conditions.

The chief executive officer must make contact with union leaders or other representatives of the work force and management to give personal assurance of commitment to the process. The CEO must obtain a commitment from union leaders and management representatives that they will support the process and should guarantee them that they will have input at the outset and on a continuing basis. The CEO must reach agreement with the leaders of employee involvement that the goals of the process include improved relationships, improved quality, increased productivity, and reduced costs.

The CEO is the only person who can effectively convey the message throughout the company that what happens in the work place has a strong correlation to what can be achieved in the market place. He or she should explain the competition, get the market share message across, explain why the customer is king, and why quality is paramount.

The CEO should endorse statistical process control as a tool for achieving quality performance and insist upon its development and implementation as a company-wide goal, as well as demonstrating a personal knowledge of the process and guaranteeing availability of resources, including training.

CEOs must take the lead in getting the message to customers and suppliers that Total Quality has been adopted as a management philosophy. They should invite personal contact if their company's performance does not live up to their commitment.

The top executives must hold themselves up as champions and leaders of the effort to achieve Total Quality and must stand ready to explain to the work force, to management, to suppliers, and to customers:

- What Total Quality means
- Why it is important

- How it will be achieved

- Why he is personally involved

- What the benefits are to the company, its customers, employees, and suppliers

Unions or other representatives of the work force must play a vital role in the quest for Total Quality and, accordingly, specific actions are required on their part.

Having received a commitment guaranteeing input, unions or other worker representatives must in turn commit to the processes of employee involvement, communications, statistical process control, and other quality performance efforts, and must keep them separate from ordinary labor relations matters. Union leaders must encourage worker support and maintain daily, active, consistent involvement. They must develop mutual ownership of the program with management.

In addition to actions required of the CEO and union leaders, actions are required at all levels of management. Absent these commitments the process will languish and ultimately fail.

All executive management must be on the same wave length as the CEO and commit to every one of the CEO's objectives, goals, and action plans. Executive management must become deputies in supporting everything in which the CEO is involved or committed. They are an extension of the CEO's office in the quest for Total Quality.

In addition to middle management's obligation to begin sharing information and authority, it has a right to extract a major commitment from executive management as the Total Quality process begins. It must be assured of unqualified support from executive management as its role changes and if indeed its overall role will diminish over time, that should be made clear at the outset.

As front-line supervisors begin to lead rather than drive, and accept and implement workers' ideas, they must receive from those above them an unconditional guarantee of support in industrial relations disputes. Anything less will undermine the entire effort.

The work force must gain an understanding that although communications, a participatory environment, employee involvement, and responsiveness to ideas are major contributors to improved relationships, they must also produce other tangible results, such as better quality, higher productivity, and lower costs. Otherwise everyone may be singing from the same hymn book but the ship could be slowly sinking.

Finally the work force has to agree to let Total Quality efforts go forth. There must be a realization that, despite past failures, programs that were fads, management's broken promises, and little likelihood of personal financial reward, the quality performance effort deserves a try.

ESTABLISHING QUALITY AS A MANAGEMENT PHILOSOPHY

A. Actions required by the chief executive officer
1. Send out a clear message that Total Quality is established as a company-wide goal—Total Quality as a way to work and manage
   a. Not *just* quality control, but rather quality performance
   b. Not *just* product improvement, but rather, productivity improvement
   c. Achieve quality in everything we do; doing the right things right (the wrongs things can also be done right); changing the way the company does things
2. Make a commitment to provide effective training with a means built in to monitor application in the workplace of what has been learned in the classroom
   a. Budget funds for training in good times and bad
   b. Establish a company-wide practice (practice—not policy) that a required portion of managers' time *will be* devoted to training—either receiving training or giving training. Managers' effectiveness in training others to become a part of performance evaluation system
3. A commitment to establish a company-wide communications program
   a. CEO to become personally *involved* in the communications process
   b. Provide resources to train people to communicate
   c. Employ every possible form of communications—in-house television, personal meetings with the CEO in plants and offices, in-house newspapers, telephone hot lines
   d. A promise from the CEO that managers *will* respond to provide two-way communications
   e. A promise from the CEO of personally finding out if people really believe that communications are effective after the process is established
4. Assurance from the CEO that the quest for Total Quality will involve all the people in the company—not just management
   a. A commitment to establish the employee involvement process throughout the company

    b. A promise from the CEO of personal involvement in the
       process
       (1) Meet with the leaders and facilitators
       (2) Speak at appropriate gatherings of teams, steering com-
           mittees, and facilitators
       (3) Demonstrate a knowledge of the process
    c. Provide requisite resources, including training, regardless of
       business conditions
    d. Establish contact with union leaders or other representatives
       of the workforce and management to give personal assur-
       ance of commitment to the process
       (1) Obtain a commitment from union leaders and manage-
           ment representatives that they will support the process—
           guarantee them that they will have input at the outset
           and on a continuing basis
    e. CEO must agree with leaders of employee involvement what
       the goals of the effort are, such as:
       (1) Improved relationships
       (2) Improved quality
       (3) Improved productivity
       (4) Reduced costs
5. The CEO is the only person who can effectively convey the
   message that what happens in the workplace has a strong correlation to what is achieved in the marketplace
    a. Explain the competition
    b. Get the market share message across
    c. Explain why quality is paramount
    d. Explain why the customer is king
6. The CEO should endorse Statistical Process Control (SPC) as a
   tool for achieving quality performance and establish its development and implementation as a company-wide goal
    a. The CEO must demonstrate a knowledge of SPC and pro-
       claim personal support for it
    b. The CEO must guarantee the availability of the requisite
       resources, including training
7. The CEO must take the lead in getting the message to suppliers
   and customers that Total Quality is adopted as a management
   philosophy
    a. The CEO should invite personal contact if the company's
       performance does not live up to its commitment
8. The CEO must become the champion and leader of the effort to
   achieve Total Quality and must stand ready to explain to the

workforce, to management, to suppliers and customers, the key elements
  a. What Total Quality means
  b. Reasons for CEO's personal involvement
  c. Why is it important
  d. How will it be achieved
  e. What will be the benefits to the company, its customers, its employees, and its suppliers
B. Actions required by unions, or other representatives of the workforce
  1. Having received a commitment guaranteeing input, unions or other worker representatives must in turn commit that the processes of employee involvement, communications, statistical process control and other quality performance efforts must, to the greatest extent possible, be kept separate from ordinary labor relations matters or disputes
  2. Union leaders or other worker representatives must agree to fill roles such as steering committee members, co-directors with management, and spokespersons for quality performance
    a. They must encourage worker support and involvement—help sell the program
    b. They must maintain daily, active, consistent involvement
    c. They must develop mutual ownership of the program with management
C. Actions required by management
  1. All executive management must be on the same wave length as the CEO and commit to every single one of the objectives, goals and actions outlined earlier for the CEO
    a. They must become deputies in supporting everything in which the CEO is involved.
    b. In a sense, executive management must become the "media for the message"—an extension of the office of the CEO in the quest for quality performance. The CEO's goals must become their action plans
  2. Middle management must recognize the critical nature of its role and realize that most failed efforts toward achieving quality performance can be laid at the feet of middle management
    a. Middle management must learn to share information with lower ranks
    b. Middle management must recognize and accept that some sharing of authority is necessary in order to develop a participatory environment

      c. Middle management must recognize its importance as a role model (good or bad) to front-line supervision and the workforce in the quest for quality performance

      d. Middle management must extract from executive management a commitment for support as it begins to share information and authority. They must be assured of a continuing role or told at the outset that their role will diminish

D. Actions required by front-line supervision

   1. A willingness, brought about through training, to become more participatory and less authoritarian—otherwise the ideas will not come forward and a vast storehouse of knowledge will not be tapped

   2. Front-line supervision must begin to implement workers' ideas, whenever possible, without reference to higher authority

   3. Again through training, front-line supervision must begin to lead rather than drive the persons whom they direct

      a. Unless union leadership and workers begin to recognize the difference between leading and managing and offer their cooperation and dedication toward "a good day's work," front-line supervision cannot abandon its role of police and enforcer and get on with leadership and participation. Unions must view it as a two-way street

   4. If front-line supervisors are to preach and practice the separation of ordinary labor relations matters and disputes from quality performance efforts, they must extract from those above them a commitment of support in industrial relations disputes

      a. Just as unions must not hold quality performance efforts hostage in labor relations disputes, middle and upper management must not sacrifice good labor relations judgment at the altar of quality performance—any gain will be short-lived and self-defeating

E. Actions required by the work force

   1. Recognizing that it is difficult to obtain any broad commitment from the workforce, as they will act primarily as individuals, it nonetheless is important to make every effort to gain certain understandings with the workforce

      a. Understanding that at the outset quality performance on their part, while vital, may mean no change in compensation ("what is in it for me"), but in the long-term productivity and quality improvement are necessary for survival

      b. Understanding that rigid work rules, strict job classifications, and strident "turf guarding" may deter quality improvement and if there is a better way it should be sought

    c. Understanding that communications, a participatory environment-employee involvement, and responsiveness to ideas, while major contributors to improved relationships, must also produce other tangible results—better quality, higher productivity, and lower costs

    d. At the end of the day the worker has to agree to let the efforts go forth. There must be a realization that, despite past failures, programs that were fads, management's broken promises, and perhaps limited if any financial reward, the quality performance process deserves a try

    e. Finally, and perhaps most difficult for the work force, fairly early on it should be mentioned that some part of hourly workers' compensation should be tied to the economic gains of business (gainsharing) while ways to eliminate production-unit based incentive systems should be sought

Building a Foundation and Installing Total Quality at Corning Glass

2

Forrest E. Behm

President, International Operations (Ret.)

Corning Glass Works

INTRODUCTION

Forrest Behm instills confidence in the leader seeking to commit to Total Quality. He provides philosophies and approaches for building a foundation and establishing Total Quality at the Corning Glass Works. Corning Glass Works is an excellent model and was selected by *Fortune Magazine* for a cover story on its leadership for Total Quality.

Behm emphasizes:

- Attitudes and Behavior
- Leadership of the CEO
- High Standards With Commensurate Training
- A Total Quality System

Tackling Total Quality at Corning Glass Works   4

Total Quality is difficult! Sometimes, for me, it has been almost impossible. Rethinking and changing my behavior so that I could achieve "error-free work" required the same effort from me as learning a foreign language. However, although it was easier to tell my associates at Corning Glass Works what they had to do for a Total Quality performance, I realized that they were experiencing the same struggle that I was. We were *all* learning a new vocabulary, a new process for our work, and were somewhat hesitant to use it, because of the fear that it might not be accepted nor be a success.

This reaction brought to mind the words of Ben Campbell Johnson in his book, *The Secret,* wherein he wrote, "When you and I were children, we wanted a better place to begin the race. . . . . I suggest you must begin where you are . . . . . where you are *geographically,* where you are *temporally,* and where you are *emotionally.* To deal with any significant decision, you begin in the *here* and *now* . . . . . and step out with faith."

Where was Corning Glass Works in the "*here* and *now?*" Corning was (and still is) a leader in glass and ceramic research, in process technology, and product quality. Our management system was effective, and we thought that we excelled in "managing" our human resources. But, in the late 1970s, our businesses were not developing as planned. We were missing our growth and profit goals. Our new products were costing too much, and our competition was becoming fierce. We were losing our lead in the businesses we had pioneered, in part, because our competitors were making more improvements in quality and service than we were.

Because of these problems, during the years 1975–1983, we were experimenting with new ways of doing work in our factories and offices. We went to the basics. More emphasis on fundamentals and less on "grand" solutions.

An example is the State College, PA factory, where we make the glass envelopes for television picture tubes. We invented the process for making what we call color T.V. bulbs, and we licensed its manufacture around the world. In the late 1970s our competitors were catching up to us and, in some cases, producing a higher quality T.V. bulb than we were. We were losing market share, and we had to act fast. We decided to concentrate on continuous job training and radical improvement in our product quality. We set two goals: (1) everyone, including plant management, would spend 5 percent, or more, of his or her time in training, and (2) we would reduce defects in our outgoing product by 90 percent. To meet the training goals, we developed courses, built training rooms in the warehouse, and trained trainers. We made training a way of life. For quality, we studied our competitors' products and carefully compared them with ours. We worked even more closely with our customers to be sure that we were concentrating on the important requirements. Then we focused our team effort on the major causes of defects and fixed the root causes. When we had met these two goals, we became fully competitive. Our service to the customer improved, our gross margin climbed, and we were once again color television bulb leaders. In December of 1987, this factory completed a major expansion of its capacity and did it ahead of schedule and below budgeted cost.

In our Greenville, OH factory, we manufacture glass parts for automotive headlights. We have been making "sealed beam" parts for forty years, and Greenville specializes in this product. In 1980, I visited a Greenville customer's general manager and asked him what he thought of our product and service. His answer was, "Well, to begin with you are arrogant. You also don't respond quickly to our questions, and you don't help us compete. In addition, your glass breaks too often in our processing." *That* got my attention! Fortunately he wanted us as a supplier and together, over several months, we developed a plan for quality. We decided what we would concentrate on, and we set tough goals without knowing how we were going to meet them. We radically increased Greenville's training. Our goal was to have everyone spend 10 percent of their time in training. We improved our communications through listening—listening to customers and to each other. We had regular exchange visits between our factory personnel and our customers. And we improved our teamwork. In two years we were meeting the quality goals we had set with our customer, we were making more gross margin, and the customer had given us a long-term contract to supply his needs.

In other factories and offices we tried group problem solving and productivity teams. In our factory in Maine we trained everyone in the use of "Quality Circles," and through their use, we eliminated missed promises and radically improved our quality.

Since all these experiments worked, Corning's top management was encouraged to do more. In April of 1983, James Houghton was elected chairman of the Board and CEO. He and his new management committee decided to make *quality* Corning's number one value. He and his committee asked me to delay my retirement in order to help them make Corning a Total Quality company: a company which would meet its internal and external customers' requirements 100 percent of the time. I was to be the Director of Quality for the Management Committee, reporting to them as a group and as individuals. I had previously worked closely with all six members of this committee, either in USA operations or when I was president of Corning International Corporation. We knew and respected each other, and we all had participated in creating the management system we were about to change. This relationship was a key to our success.

We had believed we were skilled in "managing" our people, and by the old standards I'd say we were quite good, but F. Roethlisberger's summary of Elton Mayo's analysis of typical management philosophy came uncomfortably close to describing some of what we had been doing. He said:

1. At the bottom are people called *Employees* who are supposed to conform to changes which they did not originate; to do what they are told to do, and get paid for it. Immediately over them are

2. People called *Supervisors* who again are merely supposed to uphold the policies and standards set down by those above, including

3. *Technical Specialists,* engineers, cost accountants, efficiency men, who are supposed to originate better methods of output and control, to aid

4. The *Top Management Men* who assume that the major inducement they can offer those who work for them is more pay. *Top Management* assumes that it is providing a livelihood, not a way of life; that informal groups in the factory are either "bad" or not present; that all authority comes from the top with no decisions allowed at the bottom.

Although Corning employees were not expected to check their brains at the door, their participation was not encouraged. As we progressed in changing management behavior, I was often asked in the factories, "Why did it take you so long to ask us to help?" I never had a good answer to this question, but I found that the factory worker, still, was always willing to help. I guess we managers, at times, acted as if the laboratory and management were our only sources of intellectual power. We often ignored the huge reservoir of people throughout the company who were waiting to be asked to participate.

I liked Corning's Anniversary Dinners, and so did many others. The dinner, the speeches, and the presentation of pins were recognition we enjoyed. Our yearly individual evaluation was usually welcome because it gave our bosses a chance to praise us and to help us improve our work. And, of course, we had salary reviews and, at times, promotions. These forms of recognition were useful, but they were not as powerful as if we had used frequent job-related feedback. We needed a "One Minute Management System." The authors of *The One Minute Manager,* Dr. Blanchard and Dr. Johnson, say that when "someone does something" there are three things that can happen: (1) a positive feedback, (2) a negative feedback, or (3) no feedback. No feedback is destructive, while timely positive and negative feedback help a person to know if he or she is winning and, if not, what must be done to win.

When I became the president of Corning International Corporation and participated in starting new operations around the world, I relearned the power of continuous job training. Previously, in the USA operations, I often "trained" people with the "sink or swim" technique, consequently making it impossible for jobs to get done right the first time or even the second time. It was a major behavior change in 1984, when we taught 28,000 employees the basic principles of quality. We followed that training with courses in problem solving and decision making, interpersonal skills, and statistics. For each course, the management committee participated in its development, and they were the first to attend. This corporate emphasis stimulated job-related training throughout the company.

When I accepted the job as director of quality, I knew that I had much to learn—quickly! So, I visited several companies with excellent reputations for leading people and producing quality. Everyone that I contacted was willing to share. I read the popular "quality" books and reread some "old friends." I also traveled again to Japan and Korea. I had made those trips many times in the past, but now I was learning concepts I had failed to learn before. With the participation of many people in and out of Corning, the fundamentals for our Total Quality Management System were formulated.

From the beginning of our quality effort, we encouraged all Corning Glass Works employees to participate in creating our new policies and training programs. We tested our courses in the factories and offices and used many of the employees' suggested changes. We wanted our system to belong to everyone. Ownership was an important goal.

We had to change our thinking about our factory processes because we believed that it was impractical and maybe impossible to produce products right the first time. We used sampling to control the level of defects. We agreed with our customers on an AQL—average quality level—which would typically be one-and-a-half percent defects per shipment. If we shipped our customer slightly less than one-and-a-half percent defects, we were satisfied and so was the customer. We have broken that pattern of thinking and are rigorously working toward the shipment of error-free products. When I saw a Japanese electronic product assembly line that had been running 14 months without one reject, I was impressed. I knew that such a performance had required Total Quality from suppliers, employees, machines, and management.

We were "Fixers." We had experts to fix data systems, accounting systems, and factory processes. They were good at fixing, but often the problems became unfixed. We learned that we had to put more up-front time and money into our projects so that we could prevent errors in the beginning.

Total Quality applied to all echelons and all functions of the company—not just the factory worker.

Deming and Juran say that most errors made in any organization are the responsibility of management not those who do the work. The numerous transactions and decisions being made every hour by managers in the laboratory, in engineering, in planning, in marketing, and in the Management Committee, when made "error free" determine whether or not the products and service are "error free."

The results of the changes that Corning Glass Works has made can be seen in our new "quality" vocabulary, the powerful work patterns that are being practiced, and the increased satisfaction employees receive from their jobs. Corning has also seen an increase in market share, and in 1987, a record in sales and earnings.

I am impressed with James Houghton and his team's commitment to Total Quality. They have made a good start, and they have set some far-reaching goals for 1991. They are: first, reduce major errors to one-tenth of what they were in 1986; second, have every employee invest 5 percent of his or her time in training; and third, introduce new products that have fewer defects on the first shipment and less required service than the product being replaced.

In the three years I was Director of Quality I learned that unless a leader is willing to devote the time and energy required for a company's behavior change, he or she should not start. It takes much time! I learned that written procedures and policies were seldom barriers or aids to change. Anyone can write new ones. The problem is with the management system, "It's how we do things around here." And the management system can change only through the directions and leadership of a CEO who is willing to change his or her behavior as well as the organizations'.

People in the United States can produce products and services equal to or better than anyone in the world. They just need leaders who know that and who are willing to do what is necessary to make it happen.

CEO Leadership: His Vision of the Mission and Objectives

5

The leadership energy that stimulated and guided Corning's change from the "old way" of managing to the "Total Quality Way" came from James Houghton, chairman and CEO; his top management team, consisting of two vice chairmen and three group presidents; and me, the newly appointed Director of Quality. When "Jamie" was elected chairman and CEO in April of 1983, he and his direct reports thought out, as a team, what Corning's missions would be, what its values were and should be, and agreed on a new vision for the company. During a two-day meeting in Rochester, New York, in October of 1983, "Jamie" shared this vision with Corning's Corporate Management Group, the top 130 managers from around the world, and he opened the meeting with the following speech.

Introduction to Quality

You have heard a couple of key words in the last two days, words that, hopefully, will help point the way to a new Corning Glass Works. The two words—Values and Quality—are small by themselves, but become powerful when setting a direction for an organization as talented and as rich in technology and people as we are. They become powerful when leaders such as yourselves build meaning for them into the everyday actions of people, at all levels, that make this company operate.

Yesterday, we discussed our Values and how they come together under the theme of Quality. Today, we'll talk about Quality. What it means and how it fits into our future. We have all heard Quality discussed. We have heard about Japanese Quality. We have heard Juran on Quality and heard about the Demming prize for Quality. We've also heard definitions such as "fitness for use" or "shipping products defect free . . . on time."

I talked yesterday about what Quality must come to mean for Corning Glass Works. I like the definition "conformance to the requirements of one's customers." It's simple and all-encompassing.

But there's a broader definition that may be more meaningful. That definition is: *Quality is knowing what needs to be done, having the tools to do it right, then doing it right . . . the first time.*

As I said, this broader definition may be more meaningful. It may be more useful to the lathe operator, the finishing foreman, the secretary, the salesman, the scientist, and the general manager. It has to be meaningful. We need to get all these people involved, and all the people who work with them involved, to do what must be done.

Know what needs to be done. Have the tools to do it. Then do it right . . . the first time.

Making this definition of Quality, this "vision" of Quality real, throughout the organization is essential if we are to succeed. It is key to our reaching 10 percent. And it can become the vehicle we use to resolve the conflicts that will naturally arise in changing our behavior to better reflect our values.

What will CGW look like when we achieve this goal? Let me tell you what my "Vision" looks like:

- I see a company where the word "customer" means much more than only those to whom we sell, where "customer" means those both inside and outside the company, those for whom we work and those who work with us . . . whose requirements must be understood and met so we can profitably conduct business.

- I see a company with products of such unquestioned quality, customers receive them without incoming inspection.

- I see a company that uses only those suppliers who know that Quality is more important than price.

- I see a company whose employees pursue training and education that directly translate into "doing the job right, the first time." And supervisors encouraging them to do so.

- I see a company where employee groups run their own areas, solve their own problems, with the supervisors acting as advisors.

- I see a company where union and management work as a team, knowing in the long run it is in their mutual best interests.

- I see a company where people are trusted and in turn trust each other; where whenever humanly possible, fear of job loss is only real when job performance is poor.

- I see a company where management pays as much attention to Quality plans, and their results, as it does today with budgets.

- I see a company in which each employee lives Quality as the key value of the firm, a value as unquestioned as integrity.

In my vision, the company will be a tough one, with high standards and high requirements, requirements that demand from each of us Change—not more work or working—but working differently, with a different attitude. It will not be easy. But, we must do it.

Now, one of the big questions, of course, is How? I can't answer that specifically today. But we can get started in the process and we've selected an individual to concentrate, full time, on that process.

I have asked Forry Behm to head our Quality effort—as our first Director of Quality. His sole mission is to help CGW make Quality a way of life. Some of you are probably asking yourselves "Why Forry? Why, if we're about to embark upon something totally new, are you asking one of the oldest managers in the company to drive it into the organization?" And, if you know Forry's situation, you're probably also asking "Isn't he about to retire? I thought this would be a long-term commitment?"

Let me try to answer those questions.

Forry is not only one of the oldest manager's in CGW, he's been a senior manager and officer of this company longer than anyone else in it. If you don't know him, you may have the mistaken impression that he represents the "old way" of thinking and doing. Anyone who does know Forry, though, and especially what he's been doing the last five years or so, knows different. He is one of the most forward-looking individuals in this company.

Forry began preaching Quality to me years ago. And when he became the operating manager of Electrical and Electronics in 1980, he put his words into action. It's no accident that State College, Biddeford, and Greenville have so dramatically improved their profitability. Or that each is dedicated to being a Total Quality organization. I'm not saying Forry is the only reason, but I know he was a strong catalyst.

Forry is highly respected; he will be able to "get things done" without a huge organization working directly for him. Because Forry is a believer, he will be an ideal salesman for the entire company.

What about his retirement? It is true that in spite of his youthful appearance he'll be 65 next spring. It is our policy that all officers retire no later than their 65th year. That will be true for Forry. Nevertheless, I consider Quality so important that Forry will continue in the job after he retires but with different arrangements.

Forry will officially retire in July of 1984 but he will continue in this very active role until October 1986—for three years—with part of his compensation being his retirement pay.

He will be an active employee, as I said, until July of next year. Nevertheless, to emphasize his dedication and concentration on Quality and the importance of being part of *your* team, Forry has asked and I have agreed to his resignation in December as an officer and member of the Board of Corning Glass Works.

His new position as Director of Quality will be a special one, unique in CGW, reporting not to any one individual, but to the Management Committee as a whole. Only in this way will we have the fully represented commitment and force of top management behind this undertaking.

In a minute, Forry is going to talk to you in more detail about his role, his thoughts on Quality, and how we can get started. But, let me answer, in advance, another question that will be on all your minds.

"Who's going to pay for it?" One half of you are probably thinking "There's no dollars so this is all fluff and no substance." The other half of you are probably thinking "Here we go spending dollars we don't have in the 10 percent program and we'll be asked, as usual, to squeeze more and make it up."

Well neither half is right!

While I do believe, as the books say, that "Quality is free," I also know it needs frontend funding in order for us to realize those very substantial subsequent gains that I know improved Quality will provide. I feel so strongly about this program that I'm willing to gamble with some "up-front" money.

The dollars that we need to spend between now and the end of 1985 will not be charged to you.

You are now setting budgets for 1984 and have tough goals for 1985. These should remain your targets and the dollars needed will not be a new overlay on these targets.

I am setting aside up to $4 million (it may or may not cost that) to get this program moving—to help with training, and to aid each and every unit in starting a meaningful program of its own. Some of this money will not be new money and will come from the redirection of a major portion of our education and training department towards this end. But some new money will be required.

This "upfront" money will not be charged against the 10 percent plan. Forry will tell you what the money will be used for but I can assure you that if we miss our 10 percent goal in 1985 solely because of this money, I'll take responsibility with the Board and you will not be penalized.

As I said, I feel very strongly about getting started. I'm willing to commit money under Forry Behm's guidance to get us moving. I'm even willing to bet that this "upfront" expenditure will help our 1985 performance and will not be a drain at all.

I'm delighted that Forry has accepted—with great enthusiasm I might add—this new assignment.

You'll note from the schedule that we're going to deal with Quality in two parts.

1. This morning we're going to talk about it *internally*—both together and in breakout groups.

2. After lunch we're going to hear how someone else does it. We're going to be exposed *externally* to a talk by John Jackson of IBM on how they deal with this issue.

As a kickoff to Forry's new role, I've asked him to lead us through this morning's session. I think you'll be excited by what he has to say.

One last thought: I believe Quality, our vision of it for CGW, is a tough, new direction that will change the company. It is a direction that must be pursued by everyone from the office to the laboratory to the product customer's site to the manufacturing floor. Only in this way can we hope to climb back up that mountain, and return to richness. Quality will help us reach 10 percent in 1985; it will help us return to the ranks of the great and prosperous corporations of the world.

"Jamie" made clear his determination to realize this vision of Total Quality by a commitment to change his management "behavior," by making money and resources available, and by selecting me to manage the change. He gave everyone at that meeting their "marching orders" and the full responsibility for making it happen.

When it was my turn to speak I also stressed why we had to change. I predicted what gains we would realize once we had become a Total Quality company, and outlined my plan for making it happen. I emphasized that mine was a suggested plan and that everyone there would be asked to participate in making the final plans. I considered of first importance the immediate training of all employees in Total Quality Awareness and explained in detail what the principles for Total Quality management were. I added that once the classrooms were set up, Jamie and his direct reports would be the first to go to class, and that in all future quality training Jamie would be the first student.

I have given speeches for 45 years—most of them successfully—but this was one of the best and the most emotionally charged speeches that I had ever given. Those 130 tough, sophisticated company leaders followed every word. All eyes were on me. No one moved. When I finished my talk there was an explosion of applause and cheering mixed with comments such as, "It's about time!" That created an emotional high few of us will forget. For me this was proof that our managers had long been ready to change, and they were telling Jamie just that!

The following day we formed our Quality Council. Because I wanted immediate involvement of our leaders, the Council members chosen were the senior vice president of Research and Development, then vice president of Engineering and Manufacturing, the vice president of Personnel, the vice president of Corporate Communications, the vice president of Purchasing, and the Directors of Quality for the three group presidents. As chairman of the Quality Council I lead the meetings, in which we decided, as a group, what we could do to make Corning a Total Quality company and how we would do it. Of course James Houghton participated in our decision, but he really let us be owners of the process. "Ownership" is very important. It makes "changing" easier.

The impact of these company leaders on our Total Quality System was impressive and should not be underestimated. They made it happen by taking time to participate in all the Council meetings and then by requiring Total Quality Management throughout their organizations.

We created our educational arm, the Quality Institute, without a place to teach. I managed a team to take over a floor in one of our Corning, New York buildings, and gave them the backing they needed to convert it into a first-class training facility. There was never an appropriation request. We just did it. Once the institute was located, we made a list of sixteen people whom we felt would qualify as instructors. The first six accepted the job, making the beginning faculty complete. One who accepted was the Corporate Director of Quality Control, another was a personnel controller, and another was a manufacturing manager who had been a plant manager. Fortunately, Corning was blessed with a small but outstanding corporate training and education department that trained our quality instructors creating a truly professional Quality Institute. Over time, it was necessary to increase the number of instructors, but as before, we never had a problem of convincing leaders to take this job. When one considers that the company careers of the instructors were interrupted for the two years they taught Quality, it is impressive that they did so, gladly. They were so proficient in the quality process that, in addition to teaching, they also became consultants to managers in the company who were having trouble making the Quality process work. They were the foundation of our corporate behavior change.

When our training process was underway and Jamie had attended the opening session, he did what everyone in the company had to do, that is think out what changes he had to make in his daily behavior so that he became consistent with the Total Quality principles. I reported to him and his direct reports individually. I was their consultant and helped them make the necessary changes.

Jamie's first action was to increase his contacts with all employees, worldwide, and demonstrate support and enthusiasm for Quality. He cleared a section of his calendar and scheduled trips to forty locations. These were not surprise visits. They were well planned and organized. They included lunch and dinner with employees, a tour, and a "Town Meeting" where Jamie fielded questions and got many suggestions, some strongly worded. People were impressed with his first visit; but when he came the second time with the same message and enthusiasm, they knew that Total Quality was permanent.

He put Quality at the top of every agenda for meetings and reviews. Everyone knew that you had better be ready to discuss quality
when you met with Jamie.

Another early step he took was to develop requirements with his
direct reports, the Board of Directors, and the stockholders. With each
member of his top team, he whacked out the requirements for their
jobs and then the requirements Jamie had to meet to assist them in
meeting their requirements.

The leader must change first. He can't delegate the change process to someone else. He can have someone like me help, but it is a
"do-it-yourself process." It is a difficult task. Maybe the most difficult
a CEO has to do.

The Total Quality System: Five Principles and Ten Actions

6

Top officials can achieve effective integration of the functions of management, quality, and the involvement of people through a new design of a Total Quality System. Many of these relationships were not acknowledged under department-wide quality control, but are badly needed under company-wide Total Quality.

The System can be used to provide guidance for appointing small, multifunctional quality improvement teams, for determining training and education needs, and for managing transitions from some nonproductive third-party inspector control to self-control by operators. It can also be employed to tighten standards and assure defect-free products and services.

The creation of a new Total Quality System not only provides opportunity to effectively communicate the preceding changes but also provides a unique opportunity for a company to rid itself of problems in its existing system. "Bands of steel" have existed, wrapped about major functional organizations of a company. Most every process in providing products and services and in the detection and correction of defects, involve talents from several of these functions. But the steel bands have been inhibitors. With the advent of cultures of small teams structured within the framework of the larger organizations, the Total Quality System can be used to guide the appointment of such teams.

Most large functional departments or operations publish their own policies, directives, manuals, procedures, and other instructions. In many companies they include quality activities never integrated, or updated, with other company and other department publications. The result has been unnecessary confrontation and confusion, along with unnecessary costs because of conflicting documentation. This problem can be avoided with the preparation of a new Total Quality System.

Another major concern is that responsibility and accountability for quality activities has changed considerably with the coming of company-wide Total Quality. These can be handled in the new design of a Total Quality System.

Further, the means are created to enhance the roles of some key participants in Total Quality. The Quality department manager is usually assigned a new and different role, i.e., as a company coordinator for quality, or member of the CEO's steering arm, or director of the company Quality Institute. The new Total Quality System can effectively communicate the new role.

The desired role of front-line supervisors is often not their existing role. Often they spend much time protecting their workers from misdirection from upper managers or from procedures prepared by procedure specialists with no experience with the process. We want more time spent as a teacher, a listener, a monitor, and a participant in acquiring and submitting evidence to the next successive customer. This can be communicated in a new Total Quality System.

Forrest Behm describes the new Total Quality System that he and his associates created for Corning Glass. First, they posed several fundamental questions about Total Quality to which they evolved answers. Then, with knowledge and advice from other companies already involved in Total Quality and from consultants, they decided on how they would create an awareness of Total Quality and start their journey.

The Quality Council chaired by the Director of Quality developed the elements of the first quality training course. We recognized this as a beginning of continuous Total Quality and job-skill training for all employees.

The Five Principles were:

1. The definition of quality is meeting your customers requirements 100 percent of the time. Where "customers" mean associates, supervisors, subordinates, various governmental agencies, suppliers, and those who purchase the product or services. It includes everyone you deal with in your job. Developing these requirements requires participation. The "customer" and "supplier" must cooperate in developing requirements and then commit to meeting them themselves.

2. The attitude of Total Quality is to constantly strive for error-free work. We no longer accepted delays, mistakes, missed promises, or anything that caused us to fail to meet the requirements. We were patient with people but impatient with the causes of the errors. We tried to always ask "Why did the error occur and what was the root cause?" Not "Who did it?" This was one way we helped drive out fear in our organization.

3. The management philosophy was to prevent errors from occurring. We invested the upfront time and money so that when the work was started it could be done error free. This required us to change some very fundamental management procedures, and to recognize the "fixers."

4. Our measurement was the cost of quality. We used it as a tool to identify where we should start eliminating errors and to justify the time and money needed to search out and eliminate root causes. The cost of quality includes the cost of prevention, plus the cost of detection or inspection, plus the cost of errors. Our approach was to invest more in prevention and root cause elimination so as to reduce detection and error cost.

5. We started in training with the first four principles. Then our Korean associates pointed out that we should emphasize constant improvement and innovation in everything we do. This is a very powerful principle. We encouraged everyone to be alert to ways of doing their jobs better or ways the company could do its work better. We improved our technologies of encouraging innovations.

To carry out these principles—to start the process—we required every "group" in the company to develop and carry out a quality plan. The plan consisted of 10 action steps and we expected immediate action on several of the steps. Each group could decide what to work on first with a few exceptions I will discuss later.

Before the training began, we identified in each organization the team that would develop and supervise the quality plan. We called these groups QIT's for quality improvement teams. In a factory, the QIT was normally the plant manager and his or her direct reports. In a marketing department or a staff group it was usually the ranking supervisor and the direct reports. Then QITs were trained an extra day so they could leave the course with a plan already agreed upon.

The action steps we taught are as follows:

1. *Commitment.* Each QIT constantly demonstrated commitment to Total Quality by group and individual behavior. Being the top management of their group, they were constantly "tested" by everyday events. They were wise if they told their subordinates and associates that they were striving to make the personal changes, but they couldn't do everything at once. The leaders must change behavior before the quality process can be effective.

2. *Teams.* It is the responsibility of each organization to develop and train the teams necessary to perform the work, to identify and eliminate errors, and to create the new products and services needed by the ultimate customers. The formal quality teams were: a steering committee to set policy and approve the direction of the quality process; the QIT'S to develop, carry out, and monitor the process; the corrective action teams formed to solve problems and then be disbanded; and the Corporate Quality Council formed to advise the CEO on all matters pertaining to Total Quality. Teamwork in all aspects of our business was strongly encouraged.

3. *Education and Training.* Total Quality begins and ends with education and training. We used the word "education" for learning something we had not done or learning a new job. We used training for learning how to do better the job we were doing today. We discovered that we had invested very little in training and it required a major effort throughout the company to increase the amount of training to where everyone spent 5 percent of his or her time in training every year.

4. *Measure and Display.* When problems were identified we displayed the errors as sample graphs and plotted the progress as we determined the causes and eliminated them. We expected each employee to be involved in measuring and displaying. We encouraged office workers (including the CEO) to display what he or she was working on.

5. *Cost of Quality.* Each organization was expected to calculate its cost of quality. We assured everyone that the COQ was not another control device for top management. It was not a tool for comparing one unit with another or a tool for measuring progress from year to year. We asked each QIT to use the cost of quality to help them focus on the major opportunities. We found it necessary to develop a short course for calculating and applying the COQ.

6. *Communications.* We expected each group to develop effective tools for communicating their progress. Communication was a personal responsibility of each leader. In addition, we encouraged the use of a sample newsletter as well as converting the corporate magazine to a quality publication.

7. *Corrective Action.* Each QIT developed its own corrective action system consistent with the training given during the awareness course. Additional training was often needed to make correc-

tive action effective. Each system was designed to make it easy and convenient for all employees to participate in the identification and solution of problems throughout the company.

8. *Recognition.* Each QIT developed a system of recognition consistent with the corporate guidelines. People were recognized for all activity that improved quality. Recognition was in many forms and took place in formal meetings and celebrations as well personal recognition on the production floor, in the laboratories, and in the offices.

9. *Event.* The purpose of the event is to celebrate major progress in Total Quality and to recommit the organization to the quality principles. We recommended that this be the last action step planned and that each event required top management approval for timing.

10. *Goals.* We placed goals last on the list of action steps because we believed that useful goals could be set only when all employees were trained in awareness and some problems identified. Goals were to be set for eliminating errors and for improving the Total Quality Management System.

Establishing the QITs and starting the process was similar to all major behavior changes. It had to be managed by the person in charge. The process required the leaders of each organization to stop doing many things they were formerly involved with and invest 20 percent to 30 percent of their time in making a Total Quality Management System work. Those leader managers who did not make the personal change found that their organization made no progress. "People watched their feet not what they said."

As we were completing our awareness training, we asked a sample of all employees what additional training they needed. With that information we developed three quality training courses. One in statistics, one in problem solving and decision making, and one in interpersonal skills. As with awareness training the first people to take these courses were top management. We then trained everyone worldwide. After these years of our quality journey, we set corporate goals. They were as follows:

1. By 1991, all employees will spend 5 percent of their time in training each year.

2. By 1991, each major group or department will have reduced selected major errors to one-tenth of their 1986 level. (This is

not all errors, but had to involve a significant part of each groups function.)

3. All new products introduced after 1991 had to have a better service performance and a lower defect level than the product replaced, or a comparable product if it were entirely "new."

Summary of the Total Quality Management System

Five CGW Principles of Quality—What does quality mean?

1. Meeting your *customers' requirements*.
2. Making your personal standard of performance *error-free work*.
3. Attaining error-free work through *managing by prevention*.
4. Measuring your error-free work status by the *cost of quality*.
5. Achieving constant *improvement and innovation*.

Ten CGW Quality Actions—How do we communicate the principles of quality?

1. Demonstrate personal *commitment* to Total Quality.
2. Establish quality improvement *teams* to implement Total Quality.
3. *Educate* everyone about Total Quality.
4. *Measure/display* key errors to focus on required corrective action.
5. Develop a *cost of quality* for every department.
6. *Communicate* CGW's commitment to Total Quality.
7. Develop a *corrective action* system to eliminate errors.
8. *Recognize* employees for contributions to Total Quality.
9. Plan an *event* to publicize the Total Quality effort.
10. Establish specific error-reduction *goals* for everyone.

DISCUSSION QUESTIONS

1. Managers employ controls to maintain a constant course for adherence to standards. Leaders engage people to achieve change—such as breakthrough to Total Quality conditions. What characteristics identify a leader? Can a manager be trained to become a leader?

Give examples of positions in your company that are structured for managers but should be structured for leaders?

2. To "get started," management must demonstrate changes in its attitudes and behavior to employees. This requires time and patience by management and is not amenable to scheduling. How much progress must be made by management before employees show a desire to become members of the company team for achieving Total Quality conditions? What signs from employees will indicate their readiness to become involved?

3. James Houghton was effective in communicating his visions for Corning Glass about Total Quality to his key managers. When were visions for your company presented to key managers? How effective was the communication?

4. Total Quality does not come free. Corning Glass considered Total Quality an investment, with risks, but also with potential to yield large returns on the investment. Houghton's vision was to reap long-term profitability and economic growth but he expected some short-term returns as well. As your company considers commitments, what are the expectations for both short- and long-term return on investments?

5. As quality declined across America, a majority of the well-trained, educated, and experienced quality professionals changed careers. To re-establish this national resource, where should companies look for training and education? Company institutes? Professional societies? Undergraduate colleges? Executive MBA and MBA colleges? Continuing education colleges?

Observations, Basic Beliefs, and Process Management at IBM

3

William W. Eggleston

Corporate Vice President, Quality (Ret.)

IBM Corporation

INTRODUCTION

William Eggleston supplements the guidelines presented in Part One with his philosophies about Total Quality in "Observations on The Quality Road" and with IBM's three basic beliefs on which IBM has operated for decades.

Eggleston emphasizes:

- Management philosophies
- Three IBM beliefs and five concepts for application
- The IBM improvement process
- Productivity

Observations on the Quality Road   7

OBSERVATIONS ON THE QUALITY ROAD

Doing the right things right is the basis of an industrial advantage. Customer focus, an open attitude toward employee involvement, and a defect management approach are key elements to start an organization on the improvement path. The process of putting the pieces in place to begin and extend the improvement, in my experience, follow a pattern that seems common to most of the companies with which I'm familiar. My purpose here is to share my understanding of that pattern with people who are interested in building Quality Management into their organizations.

The base from which many organizations start is characterized by the absence of essential measurements of quality as seen by its customers, the absence of regular management review, and a lack of knowledge as to the cost of the lack of quality to the organization. Most often, when asked, management of these companies will state their products are meeting customers' requirements, are as good or better than the competition's, and they would estimate the cost of quality as approximating 10 percent or less. The essential theme is that good people will do good work and there isn't management time for inspection and theme setting (and I expect this work is seen as mundane). Further, some would say that to improve their product's quality would increase its cost which couldn't be recovered in the price.

There is a variation on this base in which some companies have recognized that faith will not satisfy their customers' requirements, and they have installed control and inspection steps in their manufacturing processes to catch the defective output and cycle it into a repair process. This is a variation that produces better products at increased cost.

From these bases, some have heard the quality management story, bought into the vision, studied others' experiences and approaches, and began to put a defect management cycle in place. Learning, communicating, and task-assigning begin as the organization, at a pace usually slower than the leadership desires, begins a major change toward customer (internal and external) orientation and the realization that management really means that no level of defect is acceptable. The costs of repair, inspection, prevention, design, scrap, obsolescence, etc., come into focus as an opportunity that doing the right things right can reduce the sum of these costs, the cost of quality. This focus usually shows COQ (cost of quality) to be in a range of 20 to 30 percent of revenue. The message that change is an acceptable and necessary condition of survival starts to take on new meaning. Real, unbiased customer views are sought which lead to measurements that become the focus for improvement. Underpinning this whole thrust is the leadership awareness that defects must be measured, analyzed, tracked to source cause, where process changes must be designed to eliminate the cause and thereby improve the quality of the process output (improved yield). It becomes evident that these improvements will reduce cost, and the process will become more effective and efficient. Employee attitudes toward management improve significantly, and communication within the organization between employees and between employees and management improves significantly. The organization becomes quite humble regarding the quality of its products and the yields of its processes.

Most examples of this event evidence an initial quick reduction in defect levels and costs and the awareness that more is needed and possible. These further efforts promise still larger return but will take much longer to achieve.

Often the interest in improvement leads to the consideration and installation of statistical quality control techniques that further the improvement and bring a level of understanding of process status not previously present.

The customer attention and the activities to collect unbiased customer data will lead to the need of understanding the competitors' product quality characteristics. Comparisons become an every day habit in evaluating progress and setting improvement goals.

If the organization's processes cross departmental boundaries, management may begin to realize that departmental improvements probably do not bring the overall design improvements needed to be competitive. One approach is process management in which executive ownership (a key concept to implant in Quality Management) is assigned for these multi-departmental processes, with clear responsibility of making these processes relevant to the needs of the business through analysis, measurement, and change at the level of the whole process. This approach forces optimization on the yield of the whole process, rather than settling for the optimization of the individual parts. (The concept was first observed and generalized at IBM, based upon techniques used to manage yields in very complex, numerous step, semiconductor processes.)

This latter refinement brings executive management clearly into the game, a welcome event to the rest of the organization. However, this entrance must be done carefully so as not to disrupt or reduce the interest in the employee involvement.

The executive's focus has to be on customer considerations and defect measurements as well as the competitiveness of the process. This is information that is not usually readily available, but must be obtained through study and comparisons of both same industry information and other industry applicable situations. The latter will produce a wealth of valid comparative information, for example, order entry, backlog management, shipment, invoicing, and collection, usually have similar patterns in a number of industries that can provide the concepts to drive improvement. The idea is to look at a company that you know does a particular thing well (order handling, warehousing, and shipment at L.L. Bean, for example) and learn from them and plan change accordingly. Also, the process owner should be expected to know who is the leader in the industry and be planning change as needed to push for leadership.

These comparisons that are directed to understanding the quality of the competitor's product and the competitiveness of your process, focus the team very strongly on reducing defects and costs (yield management) and to pushing the technology of their process. And out of these efforts will emerge the importance of cycle time both in yield and cost management. The combination of highest yield and lowest cycle time produces the industry's most competitive process.

At this point, the focus must remain on customer, comparison, yield, process design, and process cycle time. Leading or not, the focus must continue if you are to compete.

Some cautions are called for.

1. Don't start this thrust unless you are prepared to stay with it from here forward. Stopping, thereby giving up your interest in quality, is not an acceptable change to your employees or customers.

2. The effort to train, initiate the organization, and generally get started will take time.

3. It requires some ongoing investment of the leader's time, not overwhelming amounts, but regular attention.

4. It calls for patience and a willingness to lead constructive and open discussions on defects and the process of designing work that gives more competitive output.

The payoff is there. In every case I have seen during my days at IBM, within months, defects were significantly down and over periods of 2 to 3 years had declined to between one-fifth and one-tenth of the initial levels. Costs moved down with the reduction of defects. And the attention to competitive comparisons brought a concern with the factors of marketplace success that has given customers better products at competitive costs. It works. It delivers competitive products and services at competitive costs.

DISCUSSION QUESTIONS

1. There exists, among many top company officials, a blind faith that investments in training and planning can be radically reduced by the employment of above average talented and motivated people. Discuss this premise.

2. William Eggleston describes three bases from which top officials start quality improvement programs. Discuss the pitfalls in starting from an unsatisfactory base and the advantages in starting from a sound base.

3. Some companies have structured and applied small teams effectively to improve quality and productivity while other companies have had inadequate experiences. Discuss IBM's concept of "Executive Ownership" as a means to achieve success. Discuss the need to "stay with it" for extended periods to make small teams work.

4. A traditional means to measure a company's quality is by internal measurements of the quality of its products and services. However, more successful top officials give priority to opinions, judgments, and measurements of customers applied to all functions of a company. Discuss how opinions, judgments, and measurements can be obtained from a customer complex.

5. Zero Defects is considered an essential requirement. It cannot be attained without a rigorous program of training and defect management. Discuss the credibility of a Zero Defects requirement. If credible, discuss the activities that must be undertaken to achieve a Zero Defects condition.

6. Discuss the value of a reputation as a Total Quality company with key Total Quality suppliers.

Total Quality at IBM: The True Productivity Driver

8

Productivity, as well as quality, has a lot of different definitions. I think of it as the relationship of investment in land, labor, and capital needed to produce a desired result. (The economists call this net contributed value.) And, I like to think that management recognizes the competitive requirement to improve productivity constantly.

We chose a simple definition for quality that would be meaningful to everyone at IBM. It is

- Meeting the requirements of our customers for defect-free products and services.

IBMers are aware that everyone has customers, either inside or outside the company, and that customer satisfaction is the key measurement of quality. It is a measurement with which everyone can identify.

Quality is everyone's job. Every individual must assume responsibility for a defect-free operation and for meeting the customer's expectations.

Let's look at the basics on which IBM has operated for decades— our three basic beliefs.

We believe that our greatest asset is our people. Our longstanding basic belief, respect for the individual, has resulted in a close working relationship of employees and management, a cooperation that has become an integral part of IBM's way of doing things.

Our personnel policies and practices reinforce the concept of respect for the individual. We strive for excellent people relations. We try to foster an environment where the interest of IBM employees and that of the corporation are closely aligned.

As a result, we have a very loyal, highly motivated, and very flexible work force, management and nonmanagement, who welcome change and who collectively pursue the remaining basic beliefs which address excellence:

- To provide our customers the best service in the world
- To pursue all tasks with the idea that they can be accomplished in a superior fashion

We have created an environment that encourages involvement. We believe everyone must be involved in the operation of the company in a meaningful way and be interested in its success. The traditional economist's measurements of productivity are of little meaning to someone working in production control, accounting, or materials distribution. Individuals monitoring quality, defects, and suggesting improvements in an *ongoing program* are a better way for them to be involved. These measurements have practical meaning. These kinds of measurements are taken as a given when quality is discussed in Japan. They barely exist in America. Five concepts make up the foundation of our quality improvement plans/strategies and activities.

People are what the first two concepts are about. Management action, beginning at the top, and the involvement of everyone are necessary conditions for improvement.

Process is the focus of the third and fourth. These two are the quality template, the keys to unlocking true operational excellence and productivity. People and process provide the necessary and sufficient conditions for improvement.

Productivity is the net of the fifth concept. We have found that quality improvement, as we practice it, is a key driver of productivity.

The concepts are relatively simple. The practice is not. The aspects of implementation take considerable management time, focus, discipline, and great attention to detail. A recent survey by the U.S. Bureau of Labor that was reported by Taylor and Wichan in "Productivity in the Banking Industry," indicated that about 60 percent of productivity improvement comes from substituting capital for labor. The remainder comes from effective management of human resource and effective job design, or as I have just said—people and process.

Don't underestimate the importance of capital investment. It sets a base for potential leadership. In the last five years, we've invested $16 billion in capital, and in the prior five years, F. T. Cary invested $11 billion. In addition, we invested $13 billion in research and development in the last five years. We've made those investments to drive our technologies and improve our competitiveness.

The efficiency of the processes with which we run the business and utilize those capital investments is a key management responsibility, and one in which we have placed the direct focus of our quality efforts. It addresses the people and process pieces of the productivity equation.

What management actions are required? Clearly, these efforts start at the top. Thomas J. Watson, Sr., made it clear when he said the entire structure of the business is built upon service to the customer in 1927.

> We believe that an organization should pursue all tasks with the idea that they can be accomplished in a superior fashion.
> —T. J. Watson, Jr.

A succession of later IBM chief executive officers have made it abundantly clear that our quality focus is not a fad,

> Our reputation for quality is only as good as our last machine or our last customer call. As IBMers none of us can be satisfied with a quality rate of 95 percent or 99 percent or anything less than 100 percent. We should expect all our products to be defect-free.
> —F. T. Cary

not the program for this year, but the way we intend to do business— today and forever.

> Quality is not the exclusive province of engineering, manufacturing, or for that matter service, marketing or administration. Quality is truly everyone's job. Each function, each individual in IBM must assume the responsibility for a defect-free operation.
> —J. R. Opel

This message is reinforced by clear policy statements, corporate directives, and numerous publications.

> We have made some real strides . . . but quality is something you have to work at every day. The moment we start to relax is the moment we fall short of the ideal.
> —John F. Akers
> March 13, 1984.

To ensure consistency in application of the quality direction, a vice president of quality was established, and a small staff was put in place to set direction and coordinate with the line management, the implementation of our increased quality emphasis.

Inspection is key. The status of product and nonproduct quality is reviewed regularly by executive management. All operating units conduct frequent detailed reviews.

Of course, when a job is well done, it should be noted. We stress recognizing improvement since it reinforces the quality activities that were utilized to achieve the gain.

We have given our management team basic awareness education to get them started. We have our own quality institutes in the United States and Belgium that develop and teach these courses. To ensure continuing progress, we provide specific courses in tools and techniques. Our education thrust recognizes the major role our people play. Only a well-informed employee can contribute the ideas, observations, and actions necessary to the continuing quality improvement of technical and business processes within the company.

We also encourage participative management—employees and managers working together. Employees working *in* the process and managers working *on* the process, both seeking to make the work activities defect-free and adaptive to tomorrow's needs. As I indicated above, IBM has spent many years putting the mechanisms of employee-management cooperation in place. The focus on work process provides one more opportunity to make the employee and his or her job more interesting and more productive. If quality improvement is to work, everyone must be involved, management (top to first line) and every employee. Management must create a participative climate if we are to get the most from our work processes.

Process is addressed by the third and fourth points:

- Focus for improvement must be on the job process
- No level of defect is acceptable

Let me share with you our process approach and what we call our quality template. We call it a template because we believe it can be placed over any process, product or nonproduct, for the purpose of defect management.

At the beginning, we started our quality improvement emphasis by focusing on products and manufacturing. By the end of 1981, our manufacturing and development locations worldwide were actively involved, and we were beginning to see significant benefits. We realized that the quality improvement techniques being applied to products would apply to every activity, to every process, in the business.

To produce a defect-free product, the design and production processes must be capable of consistently yielding the desired (defect-free) result. The same holds true for the "white collar processes." As we first looked at these, we found many very complex processes where defect-oriented measurements did not exist. Many processes were ill-defined because of constant change, and corrective actions only followed a crisis.

The processes I am referring to are common to business entities—billing, accounts receivable, personnel data systems, order entry, distribution, inventory management, just to name a few.

Few people understood these cross-functional processes as a whole. No one could speak to their capabilities, and while they generally are under accounting control and are effective as far as in the end producing a desired result, they represent a gold mine for quality improvement and resulting productivity gains.

To begin a process improvement effort, we needed common understanding. We had to define what we meant by a process. I'll simplify it as a collection of tasks to achieve a result (see Figure 1).

Being a large company, these processes crossed organization boundaries and therefore, didn't have natural management focus. To correct that, we established owners, executives with the responsibility to assure that the process meets the needs of the business and can be adjusted to address future directions. Ownership involved managing quality teams crossing organizational and geographic boundaries.

The process must be defined and analyzed—where it begins and ends; the skills its people bring to it; the information that flows through it, its structure, interfaces, and how it fits into its related business activities; and the value add it contributes.

Appropriate measurements and a process control function must be established by the process owner for control and adaptability of the process. Processes tend to adapt for comfort with their environment over time rather than stay lean and competitive. This is one reason why declining productivity sets in. People build buffers seeking to minimize the effect of external change on their day-to-day activities. It is management's job to keep resources productive. We go one step further and say it is management's job to adapt and improve the process on an ongoing basis. Improving the process, through education and training (new techniques), "best of breed" tools, and better information (procedures) helps to overcome the tendencies of processes to grow fat and the management to become complacent.

Now, let's take the process concept and discuss our defect removal cycle (see Figure 2).

FIGURE 1. PROCESS DEFINITION

The organization of people utilizing procedures, machines, and materials into work
  activities needed to produce a specific end result.
It is a schedule of activities characterized as having
  • Measureable inputs
  • Value added
  • Measureable outputs
  • Repeatable activities

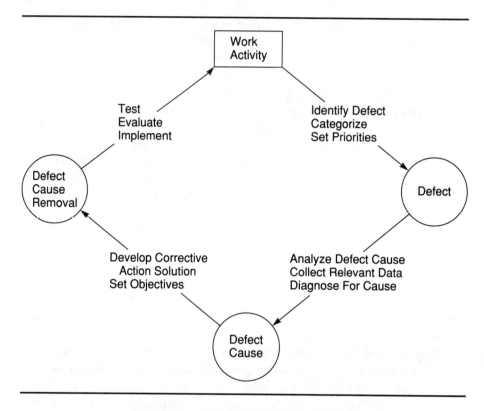

FIGURE 2. DEFECT REMOVAL CYCLE

We feel we need to bring significant focus to defect-oriented measurements. These measurements must be relevant to the people doing the work. Then, the employee is more likely to be involved in removing defects and seeing the effect in measurements. The Japanese systems of quality improvement assume measurements are in place. That is not the case here.

First, measurements should highlight the presence of defects. Using analytical means, define the defects and set priorities for cause removal. Where there are no measurements, pain and crisis initiate corrective activities. Second, determine what is causing the defects. Third, identify ways to eliminate the causes of the defects. Test and evaluate the solution prior to implementation. Finally, test and evaluate the corrective action. If it works and is not a suboptimized solution, introduce it into the process. The defect removal cycle should continue as long as defects arise for which we can assign a cause.

At each step of the defect removal cycle, a variety of tools are available for use. Figure 3 contains a partial list. There are tools to do

FIGURE 3. TOOLS AND TECHNIQUES

Defect Identification	Cause Analysis	Corrective Action	Test Evaluate
Checklists	Cause effect diag.	Particip. mgmt.	Measurements
Run charts	Scatter diag.	Statistical tools	Trend charts
Tally sheets	Frequency distrib.	Mgmt. skills	Control chart
Pareto	Vintage analysis	Consultants	Cost of quality
Control charts	Pareto/histograms		Simulation
Failure analysis	Regression anal.		Pilot programs
Particip. mgmt.	Control charts		
Department	Consultants		
act. analysis	Particip. mgmt.		
Cost of quality	Figure analysis		
	Process analysis		
	technique		
	Information logistics		
	Critical success		
	factors identification		

process analysis—for example, department activity analysis and process analysis techniques. These let you assess work within a process at the task level in terms relevant to the employee as well as the management. The statistical tools permit you to estimate when a process is in control. Other tools help in the accumulation and presentation of data. Few of these are unique to IBM. All are taught to our managers and professionals in our quality schools. It is in the defect removal cycle that the greatest value of quality teams becomes evident.

To summarize, our quality template is: *to focus on the process,* to assign ownership, and to utilize the defect removal cycle with the appropriate quality tools, including continuous measurement and ratcheting down of targets. The concept: *no level of defect is acceptable.* Figure 2 shows the effect of the defect removal cycle and the lowering of targets that happens over time.

Lastly, quality improvement reduces total costs. We have made estimates of our total quality cost. These are all the dollars we spend to ensure that our services and products meet our customers' requirements, which includes the dollars we spend to rework things that don't meet requirements or to fix things that break. We classify these expenditures in two broad categories—cost of conformance and the costs of nonconformance.

The cost of conformance includes the prevention and measures of selecting materials, education, training, procedures and systems, and tools. Appraisal includes performing audits, tests, assurance, and inspections. Together conformance and appraisal add up to about 25 percent of our total quality costs. The cost of nonconformance or failure includes all repair activity (that's an arbitrary choice), scrap and rework, engineering changes, problem determination, etc. A complete list would be very long. This is the major portion of quality cost, about 75 percent of it. Like many industrial companies, we estimate that our quality costs vary from 15 to 40 percent of the revenue stream, depending on product area.

After several years of experience, we believe that it is a reasonable expectation to reduce quality costs by half, providing a significant productivity gain. These reductions come as a by-product of the quality improvement efforts. For our company, the opportunity is measured in billions of dollars a year in increased productivity, as the quality benefits materialize. It is indeed a win-win game. We win by offering more attractive products and services to our customers, and we win because we reduced the expense to produce those products and services. Spending more on prevention to improve the capabilities of processes and utilizing the defect removal cycle dramatically reduces failure costs and therefore, dramatically reduces overall quality costs. We see leverages of over 100 to 1 in many cases.

Figure 4 is an example of finding a defect at the semiconductor device level in-house at various stages of production as opposed to dispatching a customer engineer to find it in a customer's office. The investment in prevention, removal of cause, is clearly evident.

Now, let's turn to a few examples of quality improvement.

With our 3081 large processor we saw a $5 \times$ reduction in repair actions and a $2 \times$ improvement in mean time between failure in 2 years from June 1982 to June 1984.

Our System 36, a small system, was an excellent product at general availability, but we were able to reduce repair actions by a factor of $2 \times$ over the next 12 months. (See Figure 5.)

And, a last example, six mature products were shipped from our Havant Plant in the United Kingdom. For every 100 warranty period calls in 1981, today we witness less than 18 repair actions (RAs) for the same products.

How do we improve repair actions? For new boxes, we design them to be better.

We have a corporate directive that states a new product must be better than its predecessor at the time we make it generally available to our customers. It must also be better than its competition.

Here is a comparison of processors. The new processor had to have fewer projected repair actions at general availability than the

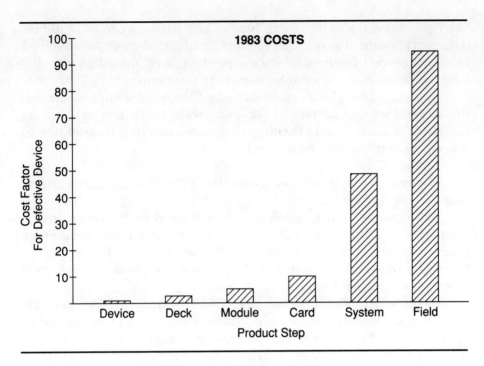

FIGURE 4.   EARLY DEFECT REMOVAL

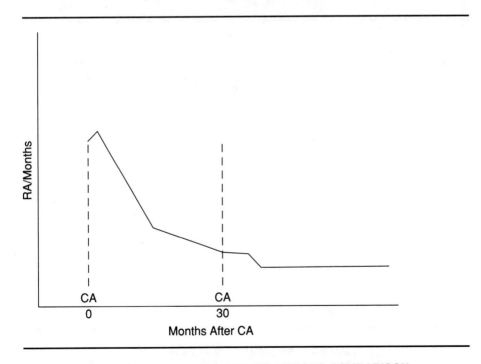

FIGURE 5.   FULL FIELD REPAIR ACTIONS COMPARISON

older processor it was replacing. Similar comparisons can be made for data entry terminal products. The old product, at most, averaged 33 months between failures. The new product is estimated to run 100 months, equal to more than 8 years, between failures.

A change brought about in our quest for quality improvement is the way we set quality targets for our products. In the past, we set targets, and after we met them, management directed its attention to other products, newer challenges.

Not so today.

If we are meeting our quality targets, it's time to make the targets tougher (see Figure 6).

For example, the technology for this product has been in the marketplace for more than 20 years. At the start of 1980, the average number of repair actions under the 90-day warranty for a selectric typewriter was meeting the target. In fact, we thought it was very good as shown by the solid line.

When we examined the quality of this product in 1980, new targets were set—targets we thought would be difficult to meet as shown by the dashed line. As you can see, we've beaten that target and repeatedly set new ones, and as a result, we're now experiencing fewer

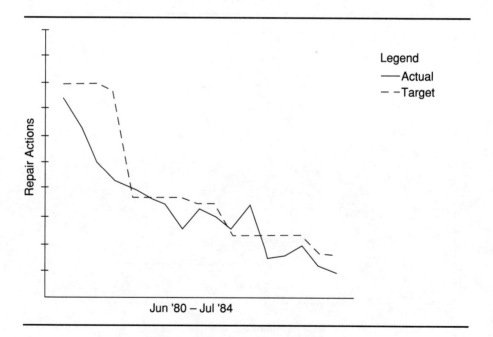

FIGURE 6. SELECTRIC III TYPEWRITER

than one-eighth the number of repair actions during the warranty period than we were just a few years ago.

This improvement comes about when product engineering analyzes defects and determine cause by reviewing specifications and the manufacturing process, and working with vendors to achieve defect-free delivery of materials, parts, and subassemblies. Training and certifying operators in their assembly jobs, more thorough testing, and greater management attention to detail play an important role. The net contributed value is increased profit, pride by the production workers in their high quality work, and greater customer satisfaction.

We manufacture a pinned board which has for years been a *back panel* for many of our processors. This particular manufacturing process has been transferred from one plant to another over the years. There's nothing exciting about it; it is not high technology, and it did not attract much attention.

In April of 1982, a bright young manager, who had recently received responsibility for manufacturing this board, decided to address this activity as a yield sensitive manufacturing process. He established a process control group, in-process measurements, and increased management attention. The results were almost immediate and dramatic (see Figure 7).

The measurements show percent of defect at final test. In April 1983, the receiving plant stopped receiving inspection for the first time in over 15 years. Currently, the experience is less than one-half percent defective at final test with the goal to continue improvement. By the way, the costs track just like the defect line. As a result, we are experiencing savings of several million dollars annually.

I showed these last examples because they are not exotic. No one had to invent anything new, they just had to focus on the basics, the process, and give attention to detail. Little things added up to a lot of improvement and significant dollar gains, which go right to the bottom line. Net contributed value is productivity.

As I indicated earlier, the same quality template is used very effectively on business processes. The results are improved output and increased productivity, both of which are essential to competitiveness.

Let me show you a few of these examples.

The general accounting department receives accounting data from the operating units and produces a consolidated statement for the company. The statements have to be produced on a specified date of every month. Of the data received, 2.8 percent had to be corrected (miscodes). Looking at this from the traditional viewpoint, 97.2 percent correct data is an A+ by many standards. With a million records

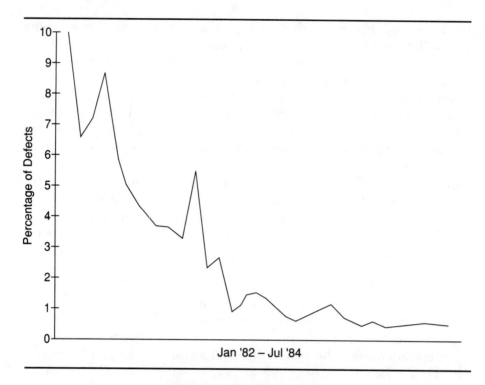

FIGURE 7. PINNED BOARD

a month, 2.8 percent error rate amounts to close to 3,000 miscodes to be corrected daily during the closing period (see Figure 8). The result was 45 percent overtime, frustrated employees, and low morale (all nonconformance costs).

The manager of the department decided to examine and improve the work process. He and his team set out to analyze the source of the defects. Targets were set and feedback was given to the operating units who provided the input data.

From March 1982 to May 1984, we see a greater than 5× reduction in miscodes, and overtime is down to around zero. The last opinion survey showed this department to have the highest morale in their group. The savings resulting from this process activity amount to more than 50 percent of the total base salaries of the department. Doing a better job with less resource is productivity.

The common release processing system is a data processing program used in every IBM factory and contains product design, test, and build information, so that the plant can manufacture the product released by the development laboratory. The problem—50 percent of the release information had to be reprocessed due to errors (see Figure 9).

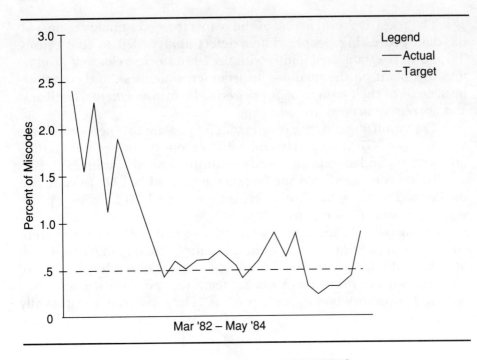

FIGURE 8.   GENERAL ACCOUNTING

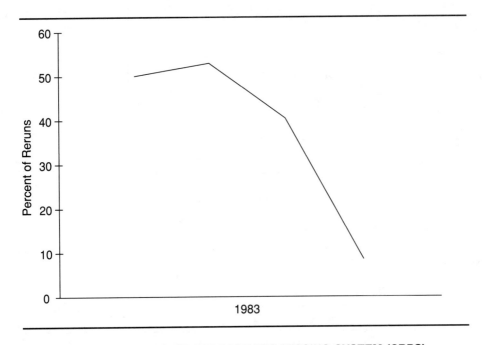

FIGURE 9.   COMMON RELEASE PROCESSING SYSTEM (CRPS)

The records group in one of the plants formed a quality team with the data processing people. Their defect analysis led to root causes. Targets were established jointly with the laboratories releasing product into this plant on the quality—its accuracy, timeliness, and completeness, etc.—of their data to be processed. The measurements, feedback, and corrective actions are ongoing.

The results: reruns are down from 50 percent to 8 percent. There are savings of $70,000 yearly and a 30 percent computer time reduction with no added expense. And the improvement continues.

"What is entered into the books, one should be able to count on the floor." Picture a distribution center handling IBM hardware products for a country (see Figure 10).

In one part of the inventory records, we had a 30 percent discrepancy, book to physical. A totally out-of-control situation that could have been brought into control by the age-old method of sending in the fire engines. But not this time. A quality team was put in place, and they analyzed inventory control as a process. They installed a statistically

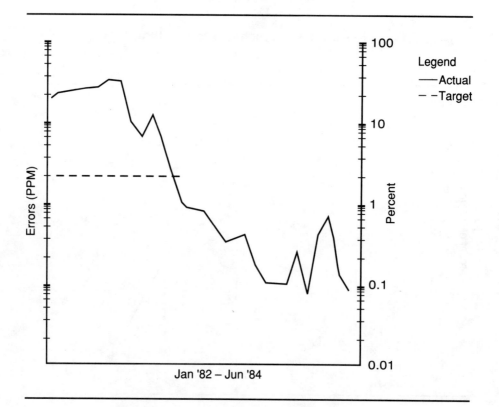

FIGURE 10.   INVENTORY RECONCILIATION

correct sample measurement taken daily. The central location took responsibility for all the inventory data processing. Error cause analysis showed improper training as a major cause. Corrective actions produced dramatic results.

In seven months, the error rate was reduced to the target set at 2 percent. Subsequently, it declined to .08 percent or 800 PPM. This is a 300× improvement! And unlike the fire engine solution, we now have a structure (a process) that is built-in, doing the job right.

Another example—when a customer places an order for software, that shipment has to match the specific hardware configuration installed in order to run the software. Occasionally, the order entry process fails to highlight this. The error rate in this process averaged between 5 and 6 percent (see Figure 11).

A team at our program information department took ownership of this process. The process was thoroughly analyzed from order entry to customer delivery. Errors were cataloged by type and location. One of the root causes was traced to 2 databases (in different divisions) that did not reconcile.

The result so far has been a 3× decrease in order entry errors. As an aside, we also discovered features that customers were using for which they had not been billed. So in addition to the increase in quality

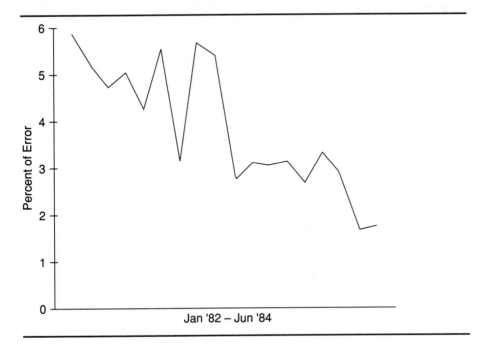

FIGURE 11.   SOFTWARE ORDER ENTRY

and productivity, we increased revenue by over $800,000 a year, and customer complaints decreased by a factor of 15.

A customer from one of our branch offices was 52 percent delinquent in paying his bills. We could not understand why a good customer would not pay his bills. The branch administration manager formed a "quality team" that included administration people from the customer, with the objective of solving the problem by removing the root cause. After appropriate analysis, it was determined that the corrective action to be taken was within our organization (see Figure 12).

The results were that delinquencies declined from 52 percent to 5 percent in the first three months. That is a $10\times$ improvement. They have remained at the 5 percent level. Branch office administration time spent with this customer was reduced from about 20 hours a week to less than 4 hours. The customer has benefitted as well. They were able to reduce the administrative time assigned to the payment of our invoices by 80 percent.

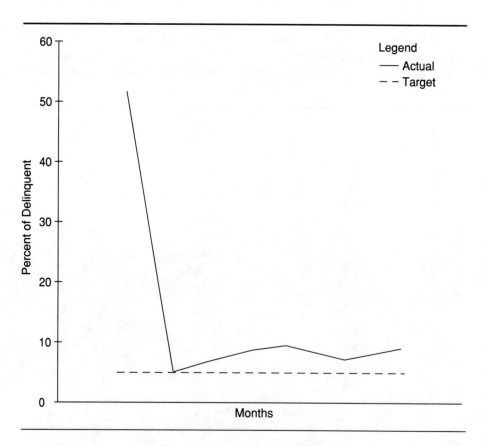

FIGURE 12.   ACCOUNTS RECEIVABLE

Our "net contributed value" consists of, first, customer satisfaction—that is hard to quantify in dollars but we all know it is meaningful; second, $18,000 in administration expense savings; third, a cash flow improvement; and fourth, we are able to extend the experiences gained to other customers, increasing their satisfaction and reducing our (and probably their) administrative expense.

These few examples are representative of what we see all across IBM. We see major improvements in all of our product lines from our 3081s down to our personal computers.

Defect identification and root cause removal are ongoing across the business. Managers are responsible for and appraised on improving the processes that they manage.

Now let me summarize where we've been and tell you where we are going.

We started with products. We know how to do that. It soon became evident (as the quality guru's had been saying for years) that the lasting gains came about by focusing on the processes that produced the products. So we did.

We reasoned that if we could remove defects from product processes and make them more productive, why not extend the same focus to other areas of the business using the same tools and techniques. So we did.

When you manage business processes, you are managing out defects and their causes from the heart and soul of the management system.

We have named executives as owners of these major processes. It is their job to understand, define, direct, and adjust the process for meeting today's expectations and to adapt the process in a timely and orderly way for tomorrow's requirements. This will ensure that our policies and practices are consistent with the capabilities of our processes. It is our feeling, based upon the productivity gains accrued from the quality emphasis so far, that increasing attention to process management is a very good investment in making resources productive today and keeping them productive tomorrow.

Isn't that your objective?

DISCUSSION QUESTIONS

1. Officials of companies seeking to commit to Total Quality are aware of the importance of small teams structured within the framework of a larger organization. IBM, Hewlett-Packard, and Texas Instruments are examples of the many companies that have structured and applied small teams effectively. But the officials know there are as many failures as successes in the development and application of

small teams. This extends to Quality Circles. What features promote success in the structuring and application of small teams? What features should be avoided?

2. Quality is the driver for improving productivity. The new, broader definition for Total Quality—from department-wide quality control to company-wide Total Quality—greatly increases the opportunities to improve productivity. Is this a major opportunity to regain eminence over foreign competitors in rates for productivity?

3. An official's objective in developing commitments must be more than acquiring status as a Total Quality company. It must be to achieve a status superior to that of existing and predicted competitors of the official's company. Benchmarks are useful criteria but there aren't enough of them. What other means can be used to acquire intelligence about competitors' resources, products, or services?

4. Is the standard of "Zero Defects" unrealistic?

5. There should be a "Quality Cost Statement" that summarizes the quality health of a company as there is a "Financial Statement" that summarizes the financial health of the company. A relationship should exist between the two. What should be included in a Quality Cost Statement?

Company-Supplier Relationships with Total Quality: From Protectionism to Partnership

4

Richard J. Pierce

Group Executive for Quality Operations (Ret.)

General Electric Company

INTRODUCTION

Richard Pierce addresses attitudes of company and supplier officials that result from typical competitions initiated by companies among their suppliers to attain the highest quality at the lowest cost in the least amount of time. He employs guides from PART ONE to substitute a partnership relationship between company and suppliers.

Pierce emphasizes:

- Attitudes
- Communication
- Leadership
- Productivity

Common Approaches for Protectionism that Require Restructure 9

Quality Control, along with the business concepts under which it usually operates, is oriented to the management of work and is insensitive to people. Relationships between a company and its suppliers involve people—many people. So a result of this lack of attention to people forms the basis for several unsatisfactory relationships. They cause risks to quality, low productivity, unnecessary high costs, and decreased ability to compete.

Unsatisfactory relationships become more apparent as we compare the purposes of Quality Control with those of Total Quality. Also, examining the structure of the interfaces between a company and its suppliers aid in identifying unsatisfactory relationships. Further, we discover them when we investigate the business concepts for operating from short-term goals and applying pressure on company officials for quick profits. This results in frequent misapplied competition placed on suppliers that generate unsatisfactory relationships. This misapplied competition encourages suppliers to short cut quality to achieve least price. At company and supplier contract negotiations, relationships are strained and contract provisions are characterized by protectionism.

The purpose of Quality Control and the purposes of Total Quality, as applied to a company's relationships with its suppliers, have major differences. The chief executive officer and the senior officials have always had the ultimate accountability for the quality of the products produced within their company and those produced by their suppliers. When products became more complex and incorporated higher technology, Quality Control was created for the primary purpose of providing "assurance" for the CEO and senior officials. By "assurance," they meant Quality Control to be a management tool to provide information and data about the quality of products produced within the company and those produced by suppliers. If failures were not prevented, were they caused by the company or a supplier and who should make the correction? Initially, the CEO gave top priority to the prevention or correction of failures that could prove catastrophic to the business of the company. Supplier officials were concerned with failures that would be catastrophic to their business. After quality costs were invented, high priority was also given to monitoring them.

Total Quality has a broader meaning and several purposes. One purpose is to create teamwork between organizations within a company that have conflicting interfaces with suppliers. Another is to substitute trust for protectionism in company-supplier relationships and to reflect this in contract provisions. An additional purpose is to replace nonproductive competition with a productive type of competition. A further purpose is to employ Total Quality as the foremost means to compete and achieve short-and long-term prosperity and economic growth for both the company and supplier. Total Quality is oriented to the performance of people in a way that generates esteem and loyalty between company and supplier. Obviously, the purposes of Total Quality breed better relationships than the singular purpose of Quality Control.

Examination of the relationships between the several organizations within a company that have conflicting interfaces with suppliers often reveal a need for restructuring the interfaces. In most companies there is an overview organization usually called a purchasing or materials organization with authority to coordinate development of contracts with suppliers. This organization's principle contribution is negotiation for price. The purchasing agents in this organization are well aware their annual adjustments to salary and promotion are related to the attainment of low prices. The members of the Quality Control organization who conduct surveillance of suppliers are equally knowledgeable that their adjustments to salaries and promotions are linked to delivery of "defect-free" products. The specialists in a manufacturing organization who negotiate delivery schedules to match company needs also know their benefits are tied to "on-time" or "just-in-time" deliveries. A root cause of adversarial relationships between these organizations and with suppliers is "rewards" are given for the wrong reason. Yet, what gets rewarded gets done. So an escalation of conflicts occurs.

Another root cause is inadequate policies for decision making about the issues of quality, price, and schedule, along with inadequate training and enforcement for these policies. That this problem still exists is usually attributable to insufficient attention by upper management. Upper managers tend to delegate the struggle for developing meaningful policies to middle level managers and in the process reduce credibility of front-line managers who are first to face such decisions. In cases where there are voids in such policies, guidance is sometimes found in a quality operations manual prepared by a procedures writer. Written policies must be strong and consistent though they may be broad in nature. However, the many day-in and day-out interpretations of policies require more detailed instructions in training programs that need to be reviewed by upper management. It needs to be well known that enforcement can be pushed upward for major decisions or repetitive issues.

The Japanese consider the issue of priorities between quality, price, and schedules as very serious. Should a new, front-line manager make a mistake in a decision involving these priorities, the mistake is corrected and the incident is chalked up to training. But, if an experienced manager makes such a mistake, it is reason for termination of employment from the company with loss of career and disgrace to the person's family.

The practice of Quality Control is usually associated with business concepts based on the pursuit of annual goals and places extreme pressure on company officials for short-term profits. They lead to nonproductive competition applied between suppliers to win contracts. Investigation often reveals that the competition is misapplied, causes duplicate and unnecessary work, and creates mistrust and protectionism between a company and its suppliers. This mistrust and protectionism can be noted both by provisions in contracts and the absence of needed provisions in contracts.

Duplicate work is caused by these unsatisfactory relationships. An outstanding example is that most companies repeat incoming inspection and tests already done by a supplier. But observation of such inspection by a company representative at the supplier's site was precluded or arranged inadequately. The supplier wanted to provide certificates of compliance in lieu of data. Or data was supplied so late that company incoming inspection and testing had to be done to meet its schedules. During further company manufacturing or assembly process, failure may occur and require failure analysis and corrective action. When it pertains to a company-made product, there is a bank of data from prior inspections and tests available that expedites failure analysis and corrective action. When made by a supplier, similar data is not available, or in unusable condition. Where high technology is a major concern to both company and supplier, separate education and training is less effective and more costly than common education and training. Sometimes unique facilities are duplicated resulting in unnecessary but significant costs. The duplication of work, the unnecessary work, along with reduction of morale, places quality at risk, increases costs, and reduces productivity and ability to compete. Total Quality creates trust and teamwork that achieves esteem and loyalty between company and suppliers as it pursues short- and long-range objectives that benefit both company and suppliers.

NEW TOTAL QUALITY RELATIONSHIPS FOR COMPETITIVE SUPERIORITY

New relationships between a company and its suppliers are needed when Total Quality is positioned as the foremost means to achieve eminence in competitions at national and international marketplaces. More specifically, the intent is to attain a superior position for the company-supplier team over that of anticipated competitors in the short-term and, particularly, in the long-term. The new relationships involve the means to integrate and strengthen the business approach to compete and achieve prosperity and economic growth for the benefit of both company and suppliers. Other new relationships are needed between scientists and engineers engaged in advanced technology, often a key element for competitiveness, and scientists and engineers from those suppliers who contribute or support the technology. As Total Quality focuses on ways to win new short- and long-range business success, new measurements are necessary.

The new relationships begin with the chief executive officer and top company officials of both the company and its suppliers. The purpose of this relationship includes informing the suppliers of the company officials' visions of the short- and long-term mission of the company and their place in it, including soliciting discussion and suggestions from the suppliers.

Other new relationships are needed between company officials who develop long-term strategic quality plans with key suppliers who may contribute important products, services, technology, special talents, processes, or facilities that are of value in formulating strategic quality plans.

For the shorter range, new relationships should occur with a company's marketing officials who coordinate the preparation of proposals for new business. The needs of a customer are frequently best met by the combined abilities of the customer and key supplier.

A vitally important issue, involving relationships of both strategic long-range quality planners and marketing officials with supplier business officials, is the accumulation of knowledge about competitors' products and services, benchmarks, and any competitive edge a competitor may have or is likely to acquire.

As long-range strategic plans frequently envision new applications of high technology—not only on the part of the company but also on the part of key suppliers—there is need for joint education and training between company and key supplier personnel. In other areas, joint education and training is more effective and less costly than if done separately. This establishes the need for new or increased relationships between company education and training officials, leaders, and instructors of a company education and training institute and supplier officials concerned with such matters.

New relationships are needed between the finance officials of a company and its suppliers. Total Quality causes many changes in measurements of quality costs. New applications of quality costs can help achieve eminence in competitiveness for many conditions when applied by both a company and key suppliers. Total Quality generates needs for upfront investments to change unsatisfactory relationships and create new relationships, followed by potential for short-term savings and then long-term prosperity and economic growth for both company and suppliers. Close relationships are needed to estimate fiscal forecasts and annual budgets.

As a company helps its suppliers to make all the changes involved with establishing Total Quality, the help often begins with teams composed of company and supplier members. This requires that new relationships be formed to arrange for such teams as well as new relationships within the teams.

Approaches for Changing Company-Supplier Attitudes and Relationships

10

- An approach to change attitudes of the chief executive officer and senior company officials.

- Preparing options to eliminate unsatisfactory relationships and fill needs for new relationships.

- An approach to change attitudes of the chief executive officer and senior supplier officials.

- Changing company-supplier relationships and preparations to make commitments for Total Quality.

Officials must improve the relationships between a company and a supplier before each can develop commitments for the many changes, described in previous chapters of this book, to establish Total Quality. Improvement begins by changing the attitudes and behavior of the CEO and senior company officials. They do much to acquire new attitudes in the process of acquiring knowledge from many credible sources and developing approaches to eliminate unsatisfactory relationships and to fill the needs for new relationships and associated measurements. They employ these approaches to provide leadership and substance for changing attitudes and behavior of the suppliers' CEO and senior officials. I draw on approaches applied successfully to a division of the General Electric Company and its 2,500 suppliers and to successful adaptations of approaches to meet the needs of other companies.

The best way to change attitudes is to acquire new knowledge that reveals superior options. Acquiring new knowledge must start with the involvement of the CEO and the senior officials who report to the CEO. Changing attitudes is a top-down process. Top officials must be role models for middle managers and they, in turn, are the examples for front-line managers, supervisors, and other employees. While changes in attitudes cannot be scheduled and involve a lengthy process, an individual who broadens perspective, acquires sufficient knowledge of particular importance, and becomes convinced a superior will sustain intent, will provide clear signs of change by his or her words and behavior.

Following a concept of Total Quality, a small team is formed to acquire the new knowledge for company officials along with material for preparing means to improve relationships with suppliers. The chief executive officer must provide leadership and direction for the team. This begins with assigning the first of a short series of missions for the team, giving a name to the team, and appointing participants to the team.

The initial mission will be to broaden perspective by acquiring knowledge of concepts and successful practices both within American companies who have achieved improved relationships and are leading the renaissance to Total Quality and within foreign companies. A likely name is "Relationships Improvement Team." It is important the chief executive officer appoint the top officials, reporting to the CEO, that are responsible for those suborganizations having direct interfaces with suppliers that are in conflict. This is often the department heads for Quality, Manufacturing, and Purchasing. The department head for Human Resources is a good addition and may add stability.

The CEO should emphasize that there are many credible sources of knowledge and that the officials of those companies that have demonstrated greatest success are those who have enlarged their perspective by investigating most of those sources. The team should be warned, however, that there are many noncredible sources to be avoided. The best sources are the board chairs, chief executive officers, and other top officials of companies who have led the renaissance to establish Total Quality, including improved relationships with suppliers, and have demonstrated success in competition in national and international marketplaces. Quality experts, who created Quality Control and counseled top officials of foreign countries on early concepts for Total Quality, are now succeeding in being heard back in American companies. Such experts as Feigenbaum, Juran, and Deming are internationally respected and excellent sources. Asian countries enjoy a high reputation for long-term and profitable relationships between companies and their suppliers. Their culture is conducive to such relationships. Officials of such foreign companies are another source for increasing perspective and learning new concepts. The application for the Malcolm Baldrige National Quality Award includes items and areas to address that involve relationships with suppliers. By their questions and identification of significant relationships, they indicate what questions the team should ask in their search. The American Society for Quality Control and the Japan Union of Scientists and Engineers are also excellent sources. In Japan, particularly, professors from prestigious universities often have close and long associations with quality activities of Japanese companies as consultants, members of the "president's audit" of quality operations, gatherers of foreign intelligence about new quality concepts, and authors of educational and training materials. The most productive means of acquiring knowledge is through interviews with the officials and experts who conceived and/or successfully applied the concepts. Tours of the American and foreign companies and exchanges of key personnel over extended time periods are good methods. Investigation of an American legacy of "programs" focusing on people involvement that have been instituted to supplement Quality Control activities is recommended. They include the Navy Department's "E for Excellence Program" that has similarities with the Japanese "Q for Quality Program." It also includes the Zero Defects Program created by the Martin Company that has features that fit the philosophies of Total Quality. The National Aeronautics and Space Administration's Award Program has common features as the Deming Quality Prize and Miles Value Engineering Award applied with Japanese companies. To begin this mission, however, it is often best to start with paper research. *Fortune* emphasizes quality by publication of a book, *Working Smarter,* sponsoring speeches from national quality leaders, and publishing feature articles on quality. *Business Week, Forbes,* and *Foreign Affairs* are other sources of articles. The publications of the American Society for Quality Control are especially useful.

During the initial mission, preparations for the second mission can be initiated. This is the categorization of suppliers into "Strategic Suppliers" and "Standard Parts Suppliers."

Although it is important for all suppliers to feel it is associated with a Total Quality team, only some categories of suppliers have significant potential to increase the competitiveness and profitability of a company and warrant investments to help them to improve competitiveness and profitability.

A team can be appointed to categorize the suppliers. Again, the approach is used to help change attitudes and perspective by involvement in acquiring knowledge. Middle managers of the organizations with conflicting supplier interfaces should be appointed to the team. The senior official responsible for strategic business planning and the marketing manager responsible for the preparation of proposals should also be members.

Indicator questions for making the two categorizations include:
For "Strategic Suppliers"

- Does the supplier provide a strategically important product, service, or resource that is critical to the long-range needs of the company?

- Is the supplier engaged in research and/or development of a complex or high technology product with obvious beneficial impact on future markets?

- Does the supplier provide products needed in the future in large quantities at significant expense but with potential for substantial future improvements in quality and productivity including substantial cost reductions in processes and/or product?

For "Standard Parts Suppliers"

- Are the supplier's products or services anticipated to be attainable from many sources in the future?

- Is the supplier a distributor of standard parts?

A completion date for the initial mission should not be given at first. The CEO is the key to progress and is concerned with both the acquisition of sufficient knowledge and signs of changing attitudes within the team. Frequent meetings need to be held with the CEO and the complete team where discussion, challenge, and debate should be encouraged about knowledge reported. A confrontational manner should be avoided at these meetings. The CEO should participate in some meetings with officials from other companies and with experts to gain first-hand knowledge. The CEO should also arrange periodic meeting between the "Relationship Improvement Team" and all other officials to both present progress reports and to generate discussion and interactions about concepts and practices learned and presented. Progress reports should also be given to newly-formed teams as part of their indoctrination. All this relates to the definition given at the beginning of this chapter that the best approach to changing attitudes is by the acquisition of new knowledge.

As new knowledge is acquired, spread, and discussed, the CEO will observe gradual changes in attitudes expressed by words and behavior, first within the "Relationship Improvement Team" and then with others. The CEO can judge when a completion date for the initial mission can be given and when it is time to assign the second mission.

The second mission is to prepare material to be presented and discussed at initial meetings with the chief executive officer and senior officials of "Strategic Suppliers."

The primary purpose of the initial meetings is to learn the attitudes of the chief executive officer and senior officials of strategic suppliers about opportunities for improved relationships. The approach used is to present visions and concepts as a base for the improved relationships yielding benefits to both the company and suppliers and then encourage open discussion to learn suppliers' viewpoints and attitudes. It is essential that company officials prepare stimulating questions that invite discussion and that will provide information about how changes will reflect suppliers needs. All of this will help add flesh and muscle to the concepts and reveal suppliers' attitudes.

Examples of discussion questions are given below. They are most effective when addressed to small groups of participants (i.e., less than thirty individuals). Additional officials can observe and support participants.

- If the concept of teamwork between company and supplier, fostered by Total Quality, were applied, what would be some examples of duplicate or unnecessary work and resources that can be eliminated or reduced?

- Is it possible to have one set of acceptance inspections and tests of supplier products at either the company's or the supplier's establishment that are conducted by a joint company-supplier team?

- Suggest long-range objectives for achieving and economic growth for both company and supplier.

- What might potential advantages be to both company and supplier if supplier personnel attended education and training courses given by the company and then for company personnel, and possibly customer personnel, to attend supplier courses?

- Is it desirable and feasible for supplier representatives to serve on company improvement teams and for suppliers to organize improvement teams that include company representatives?

- Discuss long-term ownership and stability of top officials and means of sustaining reputations and ethics for both company and supplier.

- In what ways can contractual documents that reflect protectionism be changed by provisions to reflect teamwork?

During these discussions, company officials are urged to participate but, particularly, to listen. All who attend the meeting will be
enlightened about attitudes of both company and suppliers. However,
the initial meetings are but a first step in influencing and changing
attitudes of supplier officials. Assignment of teams to supply information for subsequent iterations of visions and concepts for review and
discussion at subsequent meetings should be made.

The first need is the vision of the company's short- and long-range
missions and the place of strategic suppliers in this mission. Previous
chapters have addressed the creation of a company's mission, with
emphasis on long-range mission. We need to focus only on the place of
suppliers in the mission.

Principles that determine the place of strategic suppliers include:

- The overriding objective of a company-strategic supplier team is
  to apply jointly the management philosophies of Total Quality
  as the primary means to achieve and sustain a superior competitive position over known and anticipated competitors in the
  short range, though especially over the long range.

- The company and the strategic suppliers will support each other
  in the development of the competitive spirit and Total Quality
  changes to attain and maintain this eminent competitive reputation.

- Precedence will be given to quality over price in decisions involving the company and a supplier. However, major joint efforts shall be applied on a continuous basis to attain reasonable
  costs.

- A company and its strategic suppliers will develop criteria and
  processes that enable a strategic supplier to deliver materials
  and parts without need for incoming inspections and tests.

- A company and its strategic suppliers will determine the information and data that is to exist in a readily useful form to support failure analysis, corrective action, waivers, or other type
  dispositions.

- A company and its strategic suppliers will develop short-term
  and long-term goals that benefit both company and suppliers.
  They will avoid protectionism provisions in contracts that benefit one or the other party but not both. They will develop
  model contracts that will further their quest for competitive
  eminence as a team.

- The company encourages, but does not require, that standard parts suppliers make all the changes to establish Total Quality. The company will apply some concepts and standards that fit the philosophy of Total Quality to all standard parts suppliers.

Company officials should discuss the above examples and present a set of principles that illuminate the supplier's place in the mission at the initial meeting with supplier officials.

A different approach for a competition can be structured, applying the management philosophies of Total Quality, to create esteem, loyalty, and teamwork between the company and its suppliers. It eliminates the unsatisfactory relationships between organizations within a company that have conflicting interfaces with suppliers, substitutes trust and teamwork for mistrust and protectionism between company and supplier, and fills needs for new relationships.

This approach for a competition aligns the company and its strategic suppliers in a long-term relationship as partners who compete against other companies and company-supplier teams. The objective is not only for the company and each strategic supplier to make all the changes described in this book to establish Total Quality, but also apply the changes in a manner to attain a competitive position superior to existing and anticipated competitors. This effort can be a powerful force in accomplishing the overriding mission of the company-supplier team. That is, to employ Total Quality concepts to attain a superior competitive position over anticipated competitors will help assure prosperity and economic growth for both company and suppliers.

The first need is to develop the criteria that define "superior competitive position." This invariably requires an increase in activity to gather intelligence about potential competitors by both the company and its suppliers. Companies and key suppliers who have done so have prospered. Others have gambled. It requires constant vigilance and a continuing effort. Criteria is needed most for the long range but should also be defined for the short range. The criteria will change with the acquisition of significant new information.

The means to establish Total Quality at a company and at an individual strategic supplier is found throughout this book. Application of the changes to attain a superior competitive position is viable from information obtained from particular sources. Changing to a Total Quality System includes a search for benchmarks and the need to develop new benchmarks. It includes inspections and tests of competitors' products by the company or supplier and by independent test laboratories. Discussions with common customers about future needs is usually revealing. It further includes learning of competitors research and development activities, interests in advanced technology, and construction of unique facilities. This information is the same type that foreign competitors learned from us as they overtook us in quality and rates of productivity. In most cases, they put more effort into their search for knowledge and information than we did.

Company officials can outline and discuss this approach for competition at the initial meeting with supplier officials.

As Total Quality is elevated to part of the business and becomes the primary means to compete for future business, there is need to restructure interfaces, communication channels, and business-type relationships between company and strategic supplier.

Strategic suppliers must increase and elevate their activities to acquire information to aid in the development of goals, working closely with business-type officials of the company. This requires a different kind of interface than provided by company purchasing agents, and improved communication channels are necessary between business officials of company and strategic supplier.

As the relatively few strategic suppliers make a substantially greater contribution to a company's competitiveness than standard parts suppliers, an approach is to create a suppliers acquisition organization composed of a strategic suppliers group and a standard parts purchasing group. Purchasing agents in the second group will continue to use competitions between standard parts suppliers though with better training and with new Total Quality standards. The head of the suppliers acquisition organization must have the vision, talent, motivation, and understanding of the management philosophies of Total Quality to be effective in a role involving teamwork with strategic suppliers. Different types of strategic supplier acquisition representatives, with similar attributes, would provide continuous, direct interfaces with suppliers. Their primary function would be to assist and encourage communication between company and supplier business officials and to support them for goal setting, planning, and measurements for attaining a superior competitive position. The approach is not intended to add personnel but to engage in extensive retraining. Reduction and streamlining of the organization is desired to minimize the number of people involved in interface functions.

Communication channels between company and strategic supplier business types need major improvement. Many companies require all two-way communications to pass through a common conduit, a purchasing agent. Though unintentional, the purchasing agent is often an obstacle to communication, particularly when the purpose is exploratory. Means must be provided for direct, open, and unobstructed communication channels between company business officials and those of strategic suppliers.

Discussion of this restructuring and improvements in communication at initial meeting with suppliers always generates additional ideas about application.

Challenge, debate, and sharing of experiences at the initial meetings between company and supplier officials enables company officials to develop objectives for subsequent meetings. Invariably, such discussions, where lively exchange is encouraged but confrontation discouraged, creates many inroads to begin changing the attitudes of strategic suppliers. The company "Relationship Improvement Team," working with strategic supplier officials as needed, can develop such objectives and form teams to conduct investigations or audits to acquire information and develop findings. Some teams are within the company, some within each strategic supplier, and some joint teams.

Examples of such teams are:

- A steering arm within each strategic supplier to work with an existing company steering arm to establish Total Quality, including a superior competitive position.

- An education and training team within each strategic supplier to acquire information and findings about common courses in the advanced technologies that are associated with attaining a superior competitive position.

- A company business measurements team to work with strategic supplier officials to determine measurements for establishing Total Quality and a superior competitive position. Also to meet new needs of the CEO, Board members, business officials, and for use with customers to learn progress from Total Quality contributions for winning contracts and providing long-range prosperity and economic growth for both the company and its strategic suppliers.

- Product and service improvement teams at each strategic supplier to work with existing similar teams at the company.

As additional meetings are held, information and findings will be discussed and refined—and in the process, it is likely there will occur significant improvements in the attitudes of CEOs and strategic supplier officials and in company-supplier relationships.

DISCUSSION QUESTIONS

1. Are there direct communications between company CEO and top officials with the CEOs and other top officials of key suppliers or are all such communications channeled through purchasing managers?

2. Do the visions of mission and objectives for a company reflect benefits only for the company or do they reflect mutual benefits for the company, its employees, and its suppliers?

3. Continuous teamwork between a company and a supplier can result in major improvements in quality and productivity along with reductions in cost. This usually means selecting suppliers with probable greatest potential and discontinuing business with the many other suppliers with similar products or services. It also means eliminating or reducing competitions between similar-type suppliers that achieved cost reductions but often at a risk to quality. Compare the benefits and disadvantages in streamlining numbers of suppliers.

4. The larger companies who have won the Baldrige Award are encouraging their suppliers to commit to Total Quality. What are the benefits to a company by developing company-supplier Total Quality teams?

5. Should criteria for Total Quality status be the same for large companies and its small key suppliers?

Improving Perspective: By Past Business Leaders and Statesmen Who Employed Capitalism to Create the World's Best-Known National Economy

5

Colin W. Williams

President and CEO (Ret.)

Aspen Institute for Humanistic Studies

INTRODUCTION

Colin Williams, former president of the Aspen Institute for Humanistic Studies, introduces a new means to enhance leadership. It is taken from the world-renowned "Executive Seminars" developed by the Institute and presented for four decades. The purpose of the seminars is to improve the perspective of the individual business official who, in turn, is able to create better visions, missions, philosophies, and sets of values for the company.

Part Five addresses the change identified in Part One as Leadership. The preceding authors strongly believe the most important element of Total Quality is leadership, beginning with the CEO. As the CEO has the greatest influence on what all other company officials, managers, and workers do, then means to improve the CEO's perspective warrants the highest attention. Other officials help the CEO develop visions and, in turn, create policies for implementation. They and the company both benefit by improving their perspective as well.

The alumni of the executive seminars include several thousand board chairs, presidents, CEOs, and other company officials and senior managers, including Loughhead, Behm, Eggleston and Pierce.

There is a reasonable consensus among most that education in the humanities, as well as in a profession, is crucial in the selection of senior managers with prospects for advancement up the corporate ladder. As Total Quality is focused on the performance of people, its roots are planted firmly in the humanities. So, the other authors visited Colin Williams, participated in his executive seminars, and attended several meetings with him at the Aspen Institute to obtain counsel.

While Part Five exposes us to only a small sample of articles, they will inspire thinking and improvement in perspective. A long-range reading program complemented by seminars similar to those of the Institute is recommended.

Colin Williams contributes an outstanding means to enhance leadership. His coauthors join the alumni in awarding him our high esteem.

The questions that these readings raise for us are many. Here are four discussion starters:

1. Can the U.S. recapture its traditional values? Or, is the consumer mentality so deeply ingrained now that there is insufficient national will to pay the price of scaling back the present standard of living so that the mortgage we have placed on the future can be met?

2. Have the neo-Confucian cultures of Japan, Korea, Taiwan, and Singapore been successful because their familial tradition is more closely geared to the structural character of the high tech economy than is the U.S. culture, with its individualistic tradition?

3. Is Japan, too, now facing problems akin to ours, as it faces (for example) the pressure to become consumer oriented as a precondition for restoring the balance of trade?

4. Schumacher's famous essay on "Buddhist Economics,"—the last of our readings—may be questionable economics, but it raises questions that both the individualistic U.S. and the familial Japan may need to face if we are to regain not only a healthy economy but a sane society.

An Introductory Essay: The Rise of Capitalism: The American Triumph and the Asian Challenge

11

In his book, *The Passions and the Interests,* Albert Hirschman expresses his uneasiness with the traditional description of the rise of capitalism. That analysis "contrasted the aristocratic, heroic ideal of the Feudal Age and the Renaissance with the bourgeois mentality and the Protestant Ethic of a later era."[1]

Hirschman sees a good deal of truth in this traditional explanation, but believes that the origins of the story need to be traced further back. St. Augustine, at the beginning of the 5th century, set the basic guidelines for medieval thinking on the subject by starting with a pessimistic view of human nature, and then insisting that strict controls were needed if human behavior was to be directed towards what ought to be.

Our natural behavior, said Augustine, is driven by three lusts—lust for power, lust for money and possessions, and sexual lust. Civic virtue requires that these lusts be controlled, and in the economic sphere this means that limits have to be set on the lust for wealth.

Augustine did, however, leave open a path to the radically different modern attitude, by his view that the effects of one vice may be checked by the functioning of another. So, for example, the lust for glory and power often rises above individual desire and is directed toward the community as a whole. This, in turn, sometimes leads to limits being set on the purely private pursuit of riches in order to build up group loyalty.

That concept can be seen as a distant precursor of the famous modern concept of "the invisible hand," which ultimately brings a market harmony out of what begins as the private passion of many individuals as they set out in pursuit of wealth. If Augustine saw the private love of glory turned into public pride in the commonwealth, with the result that at least part of the wealth (to use a current phrase) could

---

1. Albert O. Hirschman, *The Passions and the Interests,* Princeton University Press, 1977, p. 4.

"trickle down," Montesquieu and Adam Smith were ready to take this positive hidden-hand viewpoint much further. Turn the individual desire for wealth loose, they counseled. Encourage a myriad of private entrepreneurs and the hidden hand, guided by the laws of supply and demand, will provide greatly increased wealth for all.

Clearly the modern viewpoint represents a basic attitudinal change of monumental proportions. Augustine and the medieval philosophers and theologians who followed him, began with a view of what human behavior ought to be—unselfish and concerned with the common good. Then, they concluded, that since our natural behavior falls far short of this, governed as it is by the three lusts, prudence requires a policy of community control over our passions and interests. Without those controls, our behavior will inevitably lead to injustice and corruption.

From the time of the Renaissance on, this mode of thinking underwent a major shift. The view of human nature became much less pessimistic. Innovators like Adam Smith then argued that if we deregulate controls over economic behavior, the energies released would work to the benefit of all.

We need to be careful in our interpretation of Adam Smith. He was aware, of course, that the search for personal wealth is, at origin, a selfish drive. Why, then, did he believe that we can profitably release it from traditional controls? It was not that he believed that the working of the marketplace would automatically transform selfish drives into benign blessings. Smith was a moral philosopher, and a decade before he wrote *The Wealth of Nations,* he wrote *The Theory of Moral Sentiments.* In it he argued that the reasons why we can be optimistic about human behavior is that we are able to recognize moral limits to our behavior. Because of that, we will recognize when our private behavior is leading to injustice. For that reason, there is no need to control our economic behavior by law, for we will recognize the need to distribute goods "as nearly as possible in the proportion which is most agreeable to the interest of the whole society."

This convenient and optimistic view of human nature did bring spectacular results. It freed enormous energies into the economy of Europe and even more into the economy of America. But, in time, major questions began to be raised as to whether regulation was needed to protect the common good. Perhaps human beings are not so made that we are sensitive to the injustices that accompany a *laissez faire* economic system. Nevertheless, Smith's basic views continue to be at the center of the arguments in favor of capitalism.[2]

---

2. The excerpt from Albert Hirschmann, included in Chapter 12, takes us a little more deeply into the process of change that led the way to Adam Smith.

So far we have looked at the modern view against the background of the Christian tradition represented by St. Augustine. The Renaissance, from which the birth of the modern age is often dated, reached back to another strand of Western thought and brought about a rebirth of interest in Greek thought, with a quite different view of human nature and of public policy in relation to property and wealth.

The classic expression of Greek thought is given in the selection from Aristotle's *Politics*.[3] But though this classical Greek viewpoint was influential in encouraging a more positive attitude to the creation of wealth, the essential ingredient that led to the creation of the capitalist economy was new—the rising trust in individual initiative, and the growing belief that the creation of wealth as the result of hard work, and the thrift which then led to the further creation of wealth, were virtues whose exercise could be expected to lead to God's blessing.

The changed atmosphere that resulted from these views was particularly evident in the new British Colonies on the American Continent. No one gave it more lively and popular expression than Benjamin Franklin in his famous piece on "The Way to Wealth," written in 1758.[4]

The nineteenth century saw enormous growth in the American economy, but by the early twentieth century, the problems of injustice on the one hand and cyclical depressions on the other, gave increasing urgency to the question of regulation. Herbert Hoover's 1928 campaign speech on "Rugged Individualism" deals with those questions.[5]

The Depression, which Hoover was unfortunate enough to preside over, did not lead to abandonment of the basic capitalist beliefs. On the contrary, Franklin Roosevelt's reforms were designed to save capitalism by fine tuning the economy along the lines suggested in Hoover's speech; by levelling out its ups and downs and by modifying its tendencies to making the rich richer and the poor poorer. Seen in that light, the story of the nineteenth century and the first half of the twentieth century, is one of capitalist economic triumph.

It is an oft-repeated theme that the U.S. economy, driven by the beliefs propounded by the Benjamin Franklins and the Adam Smiths, made remarkable strides in both productivity and quality until the 1950s and 1960s. Then, a common interpretation has it, the work ethic showed serious signs of decay, and the capital-providing tradition of thrift gave way to a culture of instant gratification, which by the 80s was spending beyond its means.

---

3. See Chapter 13.
4. See Chapter 14.
5. See Chapter 15.

There is also another oft-repeated theme, that waiting in the wings was another claimant to the productivity-quality throne. Japan is the well known claimant, pursued by Taiwan, Korea, Singapore, and Hong Kong.

What is behind this remarkable surge of the new capitalism along the Asian rim? Various explanations have been given, with one in particular gaining increasing currency. If the U.S. was in the process of losing its work ethic or, at least, losing its commitment to thrift and quality, Japan was ready, with a culture beautifully suited for the next phase of the capitalist story.

In the nineteenth century, Japan, with its belief in its own destiny to world leadership, but aware that she was not yet ready to assume her destined role, set out to discover the secrets of the Western cultures and to integrate them into her system. She made tremendous strides before being led astray by a militaristic vision of a short cut to glory—a vision that ended up in ignominious defeat.

While the militaristic version was thoroughly discredited, Japan's dream of world leadership remained intact. Why did she succeed, while the U.S. was faltering? Because, so the popular thesis runs, her neo-Confucian culture gave her the vision and the values that were needed. With its familial tradition, its emphasis on education, its strong sense of discipline, and its style of planning, it was admirably fitted for the task of developing a modern economy, with its technological complexity and its escalating demand for quality.[6]

---

6. Chapters 16 and 17, written by Morishima Michio and Frank Gibney, help us explore this thesis.

The Passions and the Interests: Political Arguments for Capitalism before Its Triumph

12

Albert O. Hirschman

Princeton University Press

Princeton, New Jersey

The earlier views on the interests and passions were subjected to several critiques. For one, as has already been shown, the proposition that man is wholly ruled by interest or self-love came to be strongly disputed. At the same time, a number of novel distinctions were made among the passions for the purpose of presenting some of them as less harmful than others, if not as outright beneficial. In this way the opposition between benign and malignant passions (with some types of acquisitive propensities classified among the former) became the eighteenth-century equivalent, especially in England, of the seventeenth-century opposition between interests and passions; but the two dichotomies overlapped and coexisted for a prolonged period.

The new line of thought was developed, primarily in critical reaction to Hobbes's thought, by the so-called sentimental school of English and Scottish moral philosophers, from Shaftesbury to Hutcheson and Hume.[1] Shaftesbury's main contribution was the rehabilitation or rediscovery of what he calls the "natural affections," such as benevolence and generosity. Distinguishing between their impact on the private and on the public good, it is not difficult for him to show that these fine sentiments serve both. Shaftesbury then addresses himself to the

---

1. Although Adam Smith was an important member of the school, his *Theory of Moral Sentiments* did not deal with the particular distinctions that Shaftesbury and Hutcheson in particular treat at considerable length. He similarly ignored the distinction between the passions and the interests.

less admirable affections or passions and divides them into the "self-affections" or "self-passions," which are aimed at, and may lead to, the private but not necessarily the public good, and the "unnatural affections" (inhumanity, envy, etc.), which achieve neither public nor private good. Within each category he further distinguishes between moderate and immoderate affections. It is interesting to watch what happens when he tries to fit economic activities into this conceptual scheme. He treats them under the rubric of "self-passions," but then proceeds to argue them out of it.

> If the regard toward [acquisition of wealth] be moderate, and in a reasonable degree; if it occasions no passionate pursuit—there is nothing in this case which is not compatible with virtue, and even suitable and beneficial to society. But if it grows at length into a real *passion;* the injury and mischief it does the public, is not greater than that which it creates to the person himself. Such a one is in reality a self-oppressor, and lies heavier on himself than he can ever do on mankind.

Obviously, then, money-making does not fit into the intermediate category of "self-passion": when pursued in moderation, it is promoted all the way to a "natural affection," which achieves both private and public good, while it is demoted to an "unnatural affection," which achieves neither, when it is indulged to excess.

Francis Hutcheson simplifies Shaftesbury's scheme and distinguishes between benevolent and selfish passions, on the one hand, and calm and violent "motions of the will," on the other. Among the few examples he gives to illustrate the latter contrast, he too cites economic activities:

> . . . the calm desire of wealth will force one, tho' with reluctance, into splendid expences when necessary to gain a good bargain or a gainful employment; while the passion of avarice is repining at these expenses.

The criterion by which Hutcheson here divides the "calm desire of wealth" (note that "calm" is the English equivalent of *doux*) from avarice is not intensity of desire, but willingness to pay high costs to achieve even higher benefits. A calm desire is thus defined as one that acts with calculation and rationality, and is therefore exactly equivalent to what in the seventeenth century was understood by interest.

There was one problem with the new terminology: while a victory of the interests over the passions could be readily visualized, language makes it rather more difficult to see how the calm passions could come out on top in a contest with the violent ones. Hume, who had also adopted the distinction between calm and violent passions, faced the matter squarely and resolved it in one sharp sentence:

> We must . . . distinguish betwixt a calm and a weak passion; betwixt a
> violent and a strong one.

In this way everything was well: an activity such as the rationally conducted acquisition of wealth could be categorized and implicitly en-
dorsed as a calm passion that would at the same time be strong and able
to triumph over a variety of turbulent (yet weak) passions. It is pre-
cisely this dual character of the acquisitive drive that Adam Smith
stresses in his well-known definition of the desire of bettering our
condition as "a desire which, *though generally calm and dispassionate,*
comes with us from the womb, and never leaves us till we go into the
grave." And a specific example of this calm but strong passion gaining
the upper hand over a violent one is given by Hume in his essay "Of
Interest":

> It is an infallible consequence of all industrious professions, to . . .
> make the love of gain prevail over the love of pleasure.

Even more extravagant claims on behalf of the "love of gain" will
be examined shortly. But, at this point of our story, Hume's statement
can stand as the culmination of the movement of ideas that has been
traced: capitalism is here hailed by a leading philosopher of the age
because it would activate some benign human proclivities at the expense of some malignant ones—because of the expectation that, in this
way, it would repress and perhaps atrophy the more destructive and
disastrous components of human nature.

Politics Chapters 8–13 13

Aristotle

8 Let us now inquire into property generally, and into the art of getting wealth, in accordance with our usual method, for a slave has been shown to be a part of property. The first question is whether the art of getting wealth is the same as the art of managing a household or a part of it, or instrumental to it; and if the last, whether in the way that the art of making shuttles is instrumental to the art of weaving, or in the way that the casting of bronze is instrumental to the art of the statuary, for they are not instrumental in the same way, but the one provides tools and the other material; and by material I mean the substratum out of which any work is made; thus wool is the material of the weaver, bronze of the statuary. Now it is easy to see that the art of household management is not identical with the art of getting wealth, for the one uses the material which the other provides. For the art which uses household stores can be no other than the art of household management. There is, however, a doubt whether the art of getting wealth is a part of household management or a distinct art. If the getter of wealth has to consider whence wealth and property can be procured, but there are many sorts of property and riches, then are husbandry, and the care and provision of food in general, parts of the art of household management or distinct arts? Again, there are many sorts of food, and therefore there are many kinds of lives both of animals and men; they must all have food, and the differences in their food have made differences in their ways of life. For of beasts, some are gregarious, others are solitary; they live in the way which is best adapted to sustain them, accordingly as they are carnivorous or her- bivorous or omnivorous; and their habits are determined for them by nature with regard to their ease and choice of food. But the same things are not naturally pleasant to all of them; and therefore the lives of carnivorous or herbivorous animals further differ among them- selves. In the lives of men too there is a great difference. The laziest are shepherds, who lead an idle life, and get their subsistence without trouble from tame animals; their flocks having to wander from place to place in search of pasture, they are compelled to follow them, cultivating a sort of living farm. Others support themselves by hunting, which is of different kinds. Some, for example, are brigands, others, who dwell near lakes or marshes or rivers or a sea in which there are fish, are fishermen, and others live by the pursuit of birds or wild beasts. The greater number obtain a living from the cultivated fruits of the soil. Such are the modes of subsistence which prevail among those whose industry springs up of itself, and whose food is not acquired by exchange and retail trade—there is the shepherd, the husbandman, the brigand, the fisherman, the hunter. Some gain a comfortable maintenance out of two employments, eking out the deficiencies of one of them by another; thus the life of a shepherd may be combined with that of a brigand, the life of a farmer with that of a hunter. Other modes of life are similarly combined in any way which the needs of men may require. Property, in the sense of a bare livelihood, seems to be given by nature herself to all, both when they are first born, and when they are grown up. For some animals bring forth, together with their offspring, so much food as will last until they are able to supply themselves; of this the vermiparous or oviparous animals are an instance; and the viviparous animals have up to a certain time a supply of food for their young in themselves, which is called milk. In like manner we may infer that, after the birth of animals, plants exist for their sake, and that the other animals exist for the sake of man,' the tame for use and food, the wild, if not all, at least the greater part of them, for food, and for the provision of clothing and various instruments. Now if nature makes nothing incomplete, and nothing in vain, the inference must be that she has made all animals for the sake of man. And so, from one point of view, the art of war is a natural art of acquisition, for the art of acquisition includes hunting, an art which we ought to practice against wild beasts, and against men who, though intended by nature to be governed, will not submit; for war of such a kind is naturally just.

Of the art of acquisition then there is one kind which by nature is a part of the management of a household, in so far as the art of household management must either find ready to hand, or itself provide, such things necessary to life, and useful for the community of the family or state, as can be stored. They are the elements of true riches; for the amount of property which is needed for a good life is not unlimited, although Solon in one of his poems says that

> No bound to riches has been fixed for man.

But there is a boundary fixed, just as there is in the other arts; for the instruments of any art are never unlimited, either in number or size, and riches may be delined as a number of instruments to be used in a household or in a state. And so we see that there is a natural art of acquisition which is practiced by managers of households and by statesmen, and the reason for this.

9   There is another variety of the art of acquisition which is commonly and rightly called an art of wealth-getting, and has in fact suggested the notion that riches and property have no limit. Being nearly connected with the preceding, it is often identified with it. But though they are not very different, neither are they the same. The kind already described is given by nature, the other is gained by experience and art.

Let us begin our discussion of the question with the following considerations. Of everything which we possess there are two uses: both belong to the thing as such, but not in the same manner, for one is the proper, and the other the improper use of it. For example, a shoe is used for wear, and is used for exchange; both are uses of the shoe. He who gives a shoe in exchange for money or food to him who wants one, does indeed use the shoe as a shoe, but this is not its proper use, for a shoe is not made to be an object of barter. The same may be said of all possessions, for the art of exchange extends to all of them, and it arises at first from what is natural, from the circumstance that some have too little, others too much. Hence we may infer that retail trade is not a natural part of the art of getting wealth; had it been so, men would have ceased to exchange when they had enough. In the first community, indeed, which is the family, this art is obviously of no use, but it begins to be useful when the society increases. For the members of the family originally had all things in common; later, when the family divided into parts, the parts shared in many things, and different parts in different things, which they had to give in exchange for what they wanted, a kind of barter which is still practiced among barbarous nations who exchange with one another the necessaries of life and nothing more; giving and receiving wine, for example, in exchange for corn, and the like. This sort of barter is not part of the wealth-getting art and is not contrary to nature, but is needed for the satisfaction of men's natural wants. The other form of exchange grew, as might have been inferred, out of this one. When the inhabitants of one country became more dependent on those of another, and they imported what they needed, and exported what they had too much of, money necessarily came into use. For the various necessaries of life are not easily carried about, and hence men agreed to employ in their dealings with each other something which was intrinsically useful and easily applicable to the purposes of life, for example, iron, silver, and the like. Of this the value was at first measured simply by size and weight, but in process of time they put a stamp upon it, to save the trouble of weighing and to mark the value.

When the use of coin had once been discovered, out of the barter of necessary articles arose the other art of wealth-getting, namely, retail trade; which was at first probably a simple matter, but became more complicated as soon as men learned by experience whence and by what exchanges the greatest profit might be made. Originating in the use of coin, the art of getting wealth is generally thought to be chiefly concerned with it, and to be the art which produces riches and wealth, having to consider how they may be accumulated. Indeed, riches is assumed by many to be only a quantity of coin, because the arts of getting wealth and retail trade are concerned with coin. Others maintain that coined money is a mere sham, a thing not natural, but conventional only, because, if the users substitute another commodity for it, it is worthless, and because it is not useful as a means to any of the necessities of life, and, indeed, he who is rich in coin may often be in want of necessary food. But how can that be wealth of which a man may have a great abundance and yet perish with hunger, like Midas in the fable, whose insatiable prayer turned everything that was set before him into gold?

Hence men seek after a better notion of riches and of the art of getting wealth, and they are right. For natural riches and the natural art of wealth-getting are a different thing; in their true form they are part of the management of a household; whereas retail trade is the art of producing wealth, not in every way, but by exchange. And it is thought to be concerned with coin; for coin is the unit of exchange and the limit of it. And there is no bound to the riches which spring from this art of wealth-getting. As in the art of medicine there is no limit to the pursuit of health, and as in the other arts there is no limit to the pursuit of their several ends, for they aim at accomplishing their ends to the uttermost (but of the means there is a limit, for the end is always the limit), so, too, in this art of wealth-getting there is no limit of the end, which is riches of the spurious kind, and the acquisition of wealth. But the art of wealth-getting which consists in household management, on the other hand, has a limit; the unlimited acquisition of wealth is not its business. And, therefore, from one point of view, all riches must have a limit; nevertheless, as a matter of fact, we find the opposite to be the case; for all getters of wealth increase their hoard of coin without limit. The source of the confusion is the near connection between the two kinds of wealth-getting; in both, the instrument is the same, although the use is different, and so they pass into one another; for each is a use of the same property, but with a difference; accumulation is the end in the one case, but there is a further end in the other. Hence some persons are led to believe that getting wealth is the object of household management, and the whole idea of their lives is that they ought either to increase their money without limit, or at any rate not to lose it. The origin of this disposition in men is that they are intent upon living only, and not upon living well; and, as their desires are unlimited, they also desire that the means of gratifying them should be without limit. Those who do aim at a good life seek the means of obtaining bodily pleasures; and, since the enjoyment of these appears to depend on property, they are absorbed in getting wealth; and so there arises the second species of wealth-getting. For, as their enjoyment is in excess, they seek an art which produces the excess of enjoyment; and, if they are not able to supply their pleasures by the art of getting wealth, they try other causes, using in turn every faculty in a manner contrary to nature. The quality of courage, for example, is not intended to make wealth, but to inspire confidence; neither is this the aim of the general's or of the physician's art; but the one aims at victory and the other at health. Nevertheless, some men turn every quality or art into a means of getting wealth; this they conceive to be the end, and to the promotion of the end they think all things must contribute.

Thus, then, we have considered the art of wealth-getting which is unnecessary, and why men want it; and also the necessary art of wealth-getting, which we have seen to be different from the other, and to be a natural part of the art of managing a household, concerned with the provision of food, not, however, like the former kind, unlimited, but having a limit.

10   And we have found the answer to our original question. Whether the art of getting wealth is the business of the manager of a household and of the statesman or not their business?—viz. that wealth is presupposed by them. For as political science does not make men, but takes them from nature and uses them, so too nature provides them with earth or sea or the like as a source of food. At this stage begins the duty of the manager of a household, who has to order the things which nature supplies—he may be compared to the weaver who has not to make but to use wool, and to know, too, what sort of wool is good and serviceable or bad and unserviceable. Were this otherwise, it would be difficult to see why the art of getting wealth is a part of the management of a household and the art of medicine not; for surely the members of a household must have health just as they must have life or any other necessity. The answer is that as from one point of view the master of the house and the ruler of the state have to consider about health, from another point of view not they but the physician has to; so in one way the art of household management, in another way the subordinate art, has to consider about wealth. But, strictly speaking, as I have already said, the means of life must be provided beforehand by nature; for the business of nature is to furnish food to that which is born, and the food of the offspring is always what remains over of that from which it is produced. That is why the art of getting wealth out of fruits and animals is always natural.

There are two sorts of wealth-getting, as I have said; one is a part of household management, the other is retail trade; the former is necessary and honorable, while that which consists in exchange is justly censured; for it is unnatural, and a mode by which men gain from one another. The most hated sort, and with the greatest reason, is usury, which makes a gain out of money itself, and not from the natural object of it. For money was intended to be used in exchange, but not to increase at interest. And this term interest, which means the birth of money from money, is applied to the breeding of money because the offspring resembles the parent. That is why of all modes of getting wealth this is the most unnatural.

11 Enough has been said about the theory of wealth-getting; we will now proceed to the practical part. Such things may be studied by a free man, but will only be practiced from necessity. The useful parts of wealth-getting are, first, the knowledge of livestock—which are most profitable, and where, and how—as for example, what sort of horses or sheep or oxen or any other animals are most likely to give a return. A man ought to know which of these pay better than others, and which pay best in particular places, for some do better in one place and some in another. Secondly, husbandry, which may be either tillage or planting, and the keeping of bees and of fish, or fowl, or of any animals which may be useful to man. These are the divisions of the true or proper art of wealth-getting and come first. Of the other, which consists in exchange, the first and most important division is commerce (of which there are three kinds—ship-owning, the conveyance of goods, exposure for sale—these again differing as they are safer or more profitable), the second is usury, the third, service for hire—of this, one kind is employed in the mechanical arts, the other in unskilled and bodily labour. There is still a third sort of wealth-getting intermediate between this and the first or natural mode which is partly natural, but is also concerned with exchange, viz. the industries that make their profit from the earth, and from things growing from the earth which, although they bear no fruit, are nevertheless profitable; for example, the cutting of timber and all mining. The art of mining itself has many branches, for there are various kinds of things dug out of the earth. Of the several divisions of wealth-getting I now speak generally; a minute consideration of them might be useful in practice, but it would be tiresome to dwell upon them at greater length now.

Those occupations are most truly arts in which there is the least element of chance; they are the meanest in which the body is most maltreated, the most servile in which there is the greatest use of the body, and the most illiberal in which there is the least need of excellence.

Works have been written upon these subjects by various persons; for example, by Chares the Parian, and Apollodorus the Lemnian, who have treated of Tillage and Planting, while others have treated of other branches; anyone who cares for such matters may refer to their writings. It would be well also to collect the scattered stories of the ways in which individuals have succeeded in amassing a fortune; for all this is useful to persons who value the art of getting wealth. There is the anecdote of Thales the Milesian and his financial scheme, which involves a principle of universal application, but is attributed to him on account of his reputation for wisdom. He was reproached for his poverty, which was supposed to show that philosophy was of no use. According to the story, he knew by his skill in the stars while it was yet winter that there would be a great harvest of olives in the coming year; so, having a little money, he gave deposits for the use of all the olive-presses in Chios and Miletus, which he hired at a low price because no one bid against him. When the harvest-time came, and many were wanted all at once and of a sudden, he let them out at any rate which he pleased, and made a quantity of money. Thus he showed the world that philosophers can easily be rich if they like, but that their ambition is of another sort. He is supposed to have given a striking proof of his wisdom, but, as I was saying, his scheme for getting wealth is of universal application, and is noting but the creation of a monopoly. It is an art often practiced by cities when they are in want of money; they make a monopoly of provisions.

There was a man of Sicily, who, having money deposited with him, bought up all the iron from the iron mines; afterwards, when the merchants from their various markets came to buy, he was the only seller, and without much increasing the price he gained 200 percent. Which when Dionysius heard, he told him that he might take away his money, but that he must not remain at Syracuse, for he thought that the man had discovered a way of making money which was injurious to his own interests. He made the same discovery as Thales; they both contrived to create a monopoly for themselves. And statesmen as well ought to know these things; for a state is often as much in want of money and of such schemes for obtaining it as a household, or even more so; hence some public men devote themselves entirely to finance.

12 Of household management we have seen that there are three parts—one is the rule of a master over slaves, which has been discussed already, another of a father, and the third of a husband. A husband and father, we saw, rules over wife and children, both free, but the rule differs, the rule over his children being a royal, over his wife a constitutional rule. For although there may be exceptions to the order of nature, the male is by nature fitter for command than the female, just as the elder and full-grown is superior to the younger and more immature. But in most constitutional states the citizens rule and are ruled by turns, for the idea of a constitutional state implies that the natures of the citizens are equal, and do not differ at all. Nevertheless, when one rules and the other is ruled we endeavor to create a difference of outward forms and names and titles of respect, which may be illustrated by the saying of Amasis about his foot-pan. The relation of the male to the female is always of this kind. The rule of a father over his children is royal, for he rules by virtue both of love and of the respect due to age, exercising a kind of royal power. And therefore Homer has appropriately called Zeus "father of Gods and men", because he is the king of them all. For a king is the natural superior of his subjects, but he should be of the same kin or kind with them, and such is the relation of elder and younger, of father and son.

13 Thus it is clear that household management attends more to men than to the acquisition of inanimate things, and to human excellence more than to the excellence of property which we call wealth, and to the excellence of freemen more than to the excellence of slaves. A question may indeed be raised, whether there is any excellence at all in a slave beyond those of an instrument and of a servant—whether he can have the excellences of temperance, courage, justice, and the like; or whether slaves possess only bodily services. And, whichever way we answer the question, a difficulty arises; for, if they have excellence, in what will they differ from freemen? On the other hand, since they are men and share in rational principle, it seems absurd to say that they have no excellence. A similar question may be raised about women and children, whether they too have excellences; ought a woman to be temperate and brave and just, and is a child to be called temperate, and intemperate, or not? So in general we may ask about the natural ruler, and the natural subject, whether they have the same or different excellences. For if a noble nature is equally required in both, why should one of them always rule, and the other always be ruled? Nor can we say that this is a question of degree, for the difference between ruler and subject is a difference of kind, which the difference of more and less never is. Yet how strange is the supposition that the one ought, and that the other ought not, to have excellence! For if the ruler is intemperate and unjust, how can he rule well? If the subject, how can he obey well? If he is licentious and cowardly, he will certainly not do what is fitting. It is evident, therefore, that both of them must have a share of excellence, but varying as natural subjects also vary among themselves. Here the very constitution of the soul has shown us the way; in it one part naturally rules, and the other is subject, and the excellence of the ruler we maintain to be different from that of the subject—the one being the excellence of the rational, and the other of the irrational part. Now, it is obvious that the same principle applies generally, and therefore almost all things rule and are ruled according to nature. But the kind of rule differs—the freeman rules over the slave after another manner from that in which the male rules over the female, or the man over the child; although the parts of the soul are present in all of them, they are present in different degrees. For the slave has no deliberative faculty at all; the woman has, but it is without authority, and the child has, but it is immature. So it must necessarily be supposed to be with the excellences of character also; all should partake of them, but only in such manner and degree as is required by each for the fulfillment of his function. Hence the ruler ought to have excellence of character in perfection, for his function, taken absolutely, demands a master artificer, and reason is such an artificer; the subjects, on the other hand, require only that measure of excellence which is proper to each of them. Clearly, then, excellence of character belongs to all of them; but the temperance of a man and of a woman, or the courage and justice of a man and of a woman, are not, as Socrates maintained, the same; the courage of a man is shown in commanding, of a woman in obeying. And this holds of all other excellences, as will be more clearly seen if we look at them in detail, for those who say generally that excellence consists in a good disposition of the soul, or in doing rightly, or the like, only deceive themselves. Far better than such definitions is the mode of speaking of those who, like Gorgias, enumerate the excellences. All classes must be deemed to have their special attributes; as the poet says of women.

> Silence is a woman's glory,

but this is not equally the glory of man. The child is imperfect, and therefore obviously his excellence is not relative to himself alone, but to the perfect man and to his teacher, and in like manner the excellence of the slave is relative to a master. Now we determined that a slave is useful for the wants of life, and therefore he will obviously require only so much excellence as will prevent him from failing in his function through cowardice or lack of self-control. Someone will ask whether, if what we are saying is true, excellence will not be required also in the artisans, for they often fail in their work through the lack of self-control. But is there not a great difference in the two cases? For the slave shares in his master's life; the artisan is less closely connected with him, and only attains excellence in proportion as he becomes a slave. The meaner sort of mechanic has a special and separate slavery; and whereas the slave exists by nature, not so the shoemaker or other artisan. It is manifest, then, that the master ought to be the source of such excellence in the slave, and not a mere possessor of the art of mastership which trains the slave in his functions. That is why they are mistaken who forbid us to converse with slaves and say that we should employ command only, for slaves stand even more in need of admonition than children.

So much for this subject; the relations of husband and wife, father and child, their several excellences, what in their intercourse with one another is good, and what is evil, and how we may pursue the good and escape the evil, will have to be discussed when we speak of the different forms of government. For, inasmuch as every family is a part of a state, and these relationships are the parts of a family, and the excellence of the part must have regard to the excellence of the whole, women and children must be trained by education with an eye to the constitution, if the excellences of either of them are supposed to make any difference in the excellences of the state. And they must make a difference; for the children grow up to be citizens, and half the free persons in a state are women.

Of these matters, enough has been said; of what remains, let us speak at another time. Regarding, then, our present inquiry as complete, we will make a new beginning. And, first, let us examine the various theories of a perfect state.

The Way to Wealth (1758) 14

Benjamin Franklin

Courteous Reader,

I have heard that nothing gives an author so great pleasure as to find his works respectfully quoted by others. Judge, then, how much I must have been gratified by an incident I am going to relate to you. I stopped my horse lately where a great number of people were collected at an auction of merchants' goods. The hour of the sale not being come, they were conversing on the badness of the times; and one of the company called to a plain, clean old man, with white locks, "Pray, Father Abraham, what think you of the times? Will not those heavy taxes quite ruin the country? How shall we ever be able to pay them? What would you advise us to?" Father Abraham stood up, and replied, "If you would have my advice, I will give it you in short, 'for a word to the wise is enough,' as Poor Richard says." They joined in desiring him to speak his mind and gathering round him, he proceeded as follows:

"Friends," says he, "the taxes are, indeed, very heavy, and, if those laid on by the government were the only ones we had to pay, we might more easily discharge them; but we have many others, and much more grievous to some of us. We are taxed twice as much by our idleness, three times as much by our pride, and four times as much by our folly; and from these taxes the commissioners cannot ease or deliver us by allowing an abatement. However, let us harken to good advice, and something may be done for us; 'God helps them that help themselves,' as Poor Richard says.

"It would be thought a hard government that should tax its people one-tenth part of their time, to be employed in its service; but idleness taxes many of us much more; sloth, by bringing on diseases, absolutely shortens life. 'Sloth, like rust, consumes faster than labor wears, while the used key is always bright,' as Poor Richard says. 'But dost thou love life, then do not squander time, for that is the stuff life is made of,' as Poor Richard says. How much more than is necessary do we spend in

115

sleep, forgetting that 'the sleeping fox catches no poultry, and that there will be sleeping enough in the grave,' as Poor Richard says.

" 'If time be of all things the most precious, wasting time must be,' as Poor Richard says, 'the greatest prodigality,' since, as he elsewhere tells us, 'lost time is never found again; and what we call time enough always proves little enough.' Let us then up and be doing, and doing to the purpose, so by diligence shall we do more with less perplexity. 'Sloth makes all things difficult, but industry all easy; and he that riseth late must trot all day and shall scarce overtake his business at night; while laziness travels so slowly that poverty soon overtakes him. Drive thy business, let not that drive thee; and early to bed and early to rise, makes a man healthy, wealthy, and wise,' as Poor Richard says.

"So what signifies wishing and hoping for better times? We may make these times better if we bestir ourselves. 'Industry need not wish, and he that lives upon hope will die fasting. There are no gains without pains; then help hands for I have no lands.' Or, if I have, they are smartly taxed. 'He that hath a trade, hath an estate; and he that hath a calling, hath an office of profit and honor,' as Poor Richard says. But then the trade must be worked at, and the calling well followed, or neither the estate nor the office will enable us to pay our taxes. If we are industrious, we shall never starve; for, 'at the workingman's house, hunger looks in but dares not enter.' Nor will the bailiff or the constable enter, for 'industry pays debts, while despair increaseth them.'

"What though you have found to treasure, nor has any rich relation left you a legacy, 'diligence is the mother of good luck, and God gives all things to industry. Then plow deep, while sluggards sleep, and you shall have corn to sell and to keep.' Work while it is called today, for you know not how much you may be hindered tomorrow. 'One today is worth two tomorrows,' as Poor Richard says; and further, 'never leave that till tomorrow which you can do today.'

"If you were a servant, would you not be ashamed that a good master should catch you idle? Are you then your own master? Be ashamed to catch yourself idle when there is so much to be done for yourself, your family, your country, and your king. Handle your tools without mittens; remember that 'the cat in gloves catches no mice,' as Poor Richard says. It is true, there is much to be done, and perhaps you are weakhanded; but stick to it steadily, and you will see great effects, for 'constant dropping wears away stones; and by diligence and patience the mouse ate in two the cable; and little strokes fell great oaks.'

"Methinks I hear some of you say, 'must a man afford himself no leisure?' I will tell thee, my friend, what Poor Richard says; 'Employ thy time well, if thou meanest to gain leisure; and since thou art not sure of a minute, throw not away an hour.' Leisure is time for doing something useful; this leisure the diligent man will obtain, but the lazy man never; for 'a life of leisure and a life of laziness are two things. Many, without labor, would live by their wits only, but they break for want of stock'; whereas industry gives comfort and plenty and respect. 'Fly pleasures, and they will follow you. The diligent spinner has a large shift; and now I have a sheep and a cow, everybody bids me goodmorrow.'

"But with our industry we must likewise be steady, settled, and careful, and oversee our own affairs with our own eyes, and not trust too much to others; for, as Poor Richard says,

> I never saw an oft-removed tree
> Nor yet an oft-removed family,
> That throve so well as those that
> settled be.

"And again, 'Three removes is as bad as a fire'; and again, 'Keep thy shop, and thy shop will keep thee'; and again, 'If you would have your business done, go, if not, send'; and again,

> He that by the plough would thrive,
> Himself must either hold or drive.

"And again, 'The eye of a master will do more work than both his hands'; and again, 'Want of care does us more damage than want of knowledge'; and again, 'Not to oversee workmen is to leave them your purse open.' Trusting too much to others' care is the ruin of many; for, 'in the affairs of this world, men are saved, not by faith but by the want of it.' But a man's own care is profitable, for, 'if you would have a faithful servant, and one that you like, serve yourself. A little neglect may breed great mischief; for want of a nail the shoe was lost, and for want of a shoe the horse was lost, and for want of a horse the rider was lost,' being overtaken and slain by the enemy; all for want of a little care about a horseshoe nail.

"So much for industry, my friends, and attention to one's own business; but to these we must add frugality, if we would make our industry more certainly successful. A man may, if he knows not how to save as he gets, 'keep his nose all his life to the grindstone and die not worth a groat at last. A fat kitchen makes a lean will'; and

> Many estates are spent in the getting,
> Since women for tea forsook spinning
> and knitting,
> And men for punch forsook hewing
> and splitting.

"If you would be wealthy, think of saving as well as of getting. The Indies have not made Spain rich, because her outgoes are greater than her incomes.

"Away, then, with your expensive follies, and you will not then have so much cause to complain of hard times, heavy taxes, and chargeable families; for,

> Women and wine, game and deceit,
> Make the wealth small, and the want
> great.

"And further, 'What maintains one vice, would bring up two children.' You may think, perhaps, that a little tea, or a little punch now and then, diet a little more costly, clothes a little finer, and a little entertainment now and then can be no great matter; but remember, 'Many a little makes a nickel.' Beware of little expenses; 'A small leak will sink a great ship,' as Poor Richard says; and again, 'Who dainties love shall beggars prove'; and moreover, 'Fools make feasts, and wise men eat them.'

"Here you are all got together to this sale of fineries and knickknacks. You call them goods, but if you do not take care, they will prove evils to some of you. You expect they will be sold cheap, and perhaps they may, for less than they cost; but, if you have no occasion for them, they must be dear to you. Remember what Poor Richard says, 'Buy what thou has no need of, and ere long thou shalt sell thy necessaries.' And again, 'At a great pennyworth pause a while.' He means that perhaps the cheapness is apparent only, and not real; or the bargain, by straitening thee in thy business, may do thee more harm than good. For in another place he says, 'Many have been ruined by buying good pennyworths.' Again, 'It is foolish to lay out money in a purchase of repentance'; and yet this folly is practiced every day at auctions, for want of minding the *Almanac.*

"Many a one, for the sake of finery on the back, have gone with a hungry belly and half-starved their families; 'Silks and satins, scarlet and velvets, put out the kitchen fire,' as Poor Richard says. These are not the necessaries of life, they can scarcely be called the conveniences; and yet, only because they look pretty, how many want to have them? By these and other extravagancies, the genteel are reduced to poverty, and forced to borrow of those whom they formerly despised, but who, through industry and frugality, have maintained their standing; in which case it appears plainly, that 'a ploughman on his legs is higher than a gentleman on his knees,' as Poor Richard says.

"Perhaps they have had a small estate left them, which they knew not the getting of; they think 'it is day and will never be night'; that a little to be spent out of so much is not worth minding; but 'always taking out of the meal tub, and never putting in, soon comes to the bottom,' as Poor Richard says; and then, when the well is dry, they know the worth of water. But this they might have known before, if they had taken his advice: 'If you would know the value of money go and try to borrow some; for he that goes a-borrowing goes a-sorrowing,' as Poor Richard says; and, indeed, so does he that lends to such people, when he goes to get it in again. Poor Dick further advises and says,

> Fond pride of dress is sure a very curse,
> Ere fancy you consult, consult your purse.

"And, again, 'Pride is as loud a beggar as want, and a great deal more saucy.' When you have bought one fine thing, you must buy ten more that your appearance may be all of a piece; but Poor Dick says, 'It is easier to suppress the first desire than to satisfy all that follow it'; and it is as truly folly for the poor to ape the rich as for the frog to swell in order to equal the ox.

> Vessels large may venture more,
> But little boats should keep near shore.

"It is, however, a folly soon punished; for, as Poor Richard says, 'Pride that dines on vanity, sups on contempt; pride breakfasted with plenty, dined with poverty, and supped with infamy.' And, after all, of what use is this pride of appearance, for which so much is risked, so much is suffered? It cannot promote health, nor ease pain; it makes no increase of merit in the person; it creates envy; it hastens misfortune.

"But what madness must it be to run in debt for these superfluities! We are offered, by the terms of this sale, six-months credit; and that, perhaps, has induced some of us to attend it, because we cannot spare the ready money and hope now to be fine without it. But, ah! think what you do when you run in debt; you give to another power over your liberty. If you cannot pay at the time, you will be ashamed to see your creditor; you will be in fear when you speak to him; you will make poor pitiful sneaking excuses and, by degrees, come to lose your veracity and sink into base, downright lying; for, 'the second vice is lying, the first is running in debt,' as Poor Richard says; and again, to the same purpose, 'lying rides upon debt's back'; whereas a freeborn Englishman ought not to be ashamed nor afraid to see or speak to any man living. But poverty often deprives a man of all spirit and virtue. 'It is hard for an empty bag to stand upright.'

"What would you think of that prince, or of that government, who should issue an edict forbidding you to dress like a gentleman or gentlewoman, on pain of imprisonment or servitude? Would you not say that you were free, have a right to dress as you please, and that such an edict would be a breach of your privileges, and such a government tyrannical? And yet you are about to put yourself under that tyranny, when you run in debt for such dress! Your creditor has authority, at his pleasure, to deprive you of your liberty by confining you in gaol for life, or by selling you for a servant, if you should not be able to pay him.

"When you have got your bargain, you may, perhaps, think little of payment; but, as Poor Richard says, 'Creditors have better memories than debtors; creditors are a superstitious sect, great observers of set days and times.' The day comes round before you are aware, and the demand is made before you are prepared to satisfy it; or, if you bear your debt in mind, the term, which at first seemed so long, will, as it lessens, appear extremely short—time will seem to have added wings to his heels as well as his shoulders. 'Those have a short Lent who owe money to be paid at Easter.' At present, perhaps, you may think yourselves in thriving circumstances, and that you can bear a little extravagance without injury; but

> For age and want save while you may,
> No morning sun lasts a whole day.

"Gain may be temporary and uncertain, but ever, while you live, expense is constant and certain; and, 'it is easier to build two chimneys than to keep one in fuel,' as Poor Richard says; so 'rather go to bed supperless than rise in debt.'

> Get what you can, and what you
> get hold,
> 'Tis the stone that will turn all your lead
> into gold.

"And when you have got the philosopher's stone, sure you will no longer complain of bad times, or the difficulty of paying taxes.

"This doctrine, my friends, is reason and wisdom; but, after all, do not depend too much upon your own industry and frugality and prudence, though excellent things; for they may all be blasted, without the blessing of heaven. And, therefore, ask that blessing humbly, and be not uncharitable to those that at present seem to want it, but comfort and help them. Remember Job suffered and was afterward prosperous.

"And now, to conclude, 'experience keeps a dear school, but fools will learn in no other,' as Poor Richard says, and scarce in that; for, it is true, 'We may give advice, but we cannot give conduct'; however, remember this, 'They that will not be counseled cannot be helped'; and further, that 'if you will not hear reason she will surely rap your knuckles,' as Poor Richard says."

Thus the old gentleman ended his harangue. The people heard it and approved the doctrine and immediately practiced the contrary, just as if it had been a common sermon; for the auction opened and they began to buy extravagantly.

I found the good man had thoroughly studied my almanacs and digested all I had dropped on those topics during the course of twenty-five years. The frequent mention he made of me must have tired anyone else; but my vanity was wonderfully delighted with it, though I was conscious that not a tenth part of the wisdom was my own, which he ascribed to me but rather the gleanings that I had made of the sense of all ages and nations. However, I resolved to be the better for the echo of it; and, though I had at first determined to buy stuff for a new coat, I went away, resolved to wear my old one a little longer. Reader, if thou wilt do the same, thy profit will be as great as mine.

Rugged Individualism (1928) 15

Herbert Hoover

A Campaign Speech

The campaign now draws near a close. The platforms of the two parties defining principles and offering solutions of various national problems have been presented and are being earnestly considered by our people.

After four months' debate it is not the Republican Party which finds reason for abandonment of any of the principles it has laid down or of the views it has expressed for solution of the problems before the country. The principles to which it adheres are rooted deeply in the foundations of our national life. The solutions which it proposes are based on experience with government and on a consciousness that it may have the responsibility for placing those solutions in action. . . .

When the war closed, the most vital of all issues both in our own country and throughout the world was whether governments should continue their wartime ownership and operation of many instrumentalities of production and distribution. We were challenged with a peacetime choice between the American system of rugged individualism and a European philosophy of diametrically opposed doctrines—doctrines of paternalism and state socialism. The acceptance of these ideas would have meant the destruction of self-government through centralization of government. It would have meant the undermining of the individual initiative and enterprise through which our people have grown to unparalleled greatness.

The Republican Party from the beginning resolutely turned its face away from these ideas and these war practices. A Republican Congress cooperated with the Democratic administration to demobilize many of our war activities. At that time the two parties were in accord upon that point. When the Republican Party came into full power, it went at once resolutely back to our fundamental conception of the state and the rights and responsibilities of the individual. Thereby it restored confidence and hope in the American people, it freed and stimulated enterprise, it restored the government to its position as an umpire instead of a player in the economic game. For these reasons the American people have gone forward in progress while the rest of the world has halted, and some countries have even gone backward. If anyone will study the causes of retarded recuperation in Europe, he will find much of it due to stifling of private initiative, on one hand, and overloading of the government with business, on the other.

There has been revived in this campaign, however, a series of proposals which, if adopted, would be a long step toward the abandonment of our American system and a surrender to the destructive operation of governmental conduct of commercial business. Because the country is faced with difficulty and doubt over certain national problems—that is, Prohibition, farm relief, and electrical power—our opponents propose that we must thrust government a long way into the businesses which give rise to these problems. In effect, they abandon the tenets of their own party and turn to state socialism as a solution for the difficulties presented by all three. It is proposed that we shall change from Prohibition to the state purchase and sale of liquor. If their agricultural relief program means anything, it means that the government shall directly or indirectly buy and sell and fix prices of agricultural products. And we are to go into the hydroelectric power business. In other words, we are confronted with a huge program of government in business.

There is, therefore, submitted to the American people a question of fundamental principle. That is: Shall we depart from the principles of our American political and economic system, upon which we have advanced beyond all the rest of the world, in order to adopt methods based on principles destructive of its very foundations? And I wish to emphasize the seriousness of these proposals. I wish to make my position clear; for this goes to the very roots of American life and progress.

I should like to state to you the effect that this projection of government in business would have upon our system of self-government and our economic system. That effect would reach to the daily life of every man and woman. It would impair the very basis of liberty and freedom, not only for those left outside the fold of expanded bureaucracy but for those embraced within it.

Let us first see the effect upon self-government. When the federal government undertakes to go into commercial business it must at once set up the organization and administration of that business, and it immediately finds itself in a labyrinth, every alley of which leads to the destruction of self-government. Commercial business requires a concentration of responsibility. Self-government requires decentralization and many checks and balances to safeguard liberty. Our government to succeed in business would need become in effect a despotism. There at once begins the destruction of self-government.

The first problem of the government about to adventure in commercial business is to determine a method of administration. It must secure leadership and direction. Shall this leadership be chosen by political agencies or shall we make it elective? The hard, practical fact is that leadership in business must come through the sheer rise in ability and character. That rise can only take place in the free atmosphere of competition. Competition is closed by bureaucracy. Political agencies are feeble channels through which to select able leaders to conduct commercial business.

Government, in order to avoid the possible incompetence, corruption, and tyranny of too great authority in individuals entrusted with commercial business, inevitably turns to boards and commissions. To make sure that there are checks and balances, each member of such boards and commissions must have equal authority. Each has his separate responsibility to the public, and at once we have the conflict of ideas and the lack of decision which would ruin any commercial business. It has contributed greatly to the demoralization of our shipping business. Moreover, these commissions must be representative of different sections and different political parties, so that at once we have an entire blight upon coordinated action within their ranks which destroys any possibility of effective administration.

Moreover, our legislative bodies cannot in fact delegate their full authority to commissions or to individuals for the conduct of matters vital to the American people; for if we would preserve government by the people we must preserve the authority of our legislators in the activities of our government.

Thus, every time the federal government goes into a commercial business, 531 senators and congressmen become the actual board of directors of that business. Every time a state government goes into business, 100 or 200 state senators and legislators become the actual directors of that business. Even if they were supermen and if there were not politics in the United States, no body of such members could competently direct commercial activities; for that requires initiative, instant decision, and action. It took Congress six years of constant discussion to even decide what the method of administration of Muscle Shoals should be.

When the federal government undertakes to go into business, the state governments are at once deprived of control and taxation of that business; when a state government undertakes to go into business, it at once deprives the municipalities of taxation and control of that business. Municipalities, being local and close to the people, can, at times, succeed in business where federal and state governments must fail. We have trouble enough with logrolling in legislative bodies today. It originates naturally from desires of citizens to advance their particular section or to secure some necessary service. It would be multiplied a thousandfold were the federal and state governments in these businesses.

The effect upon our economic progress would be even worse. Business progressiveness is dependent on competition. New methods and new ideas are the outgrowth of the spirit of adventure, of individual initiative, and of individual enterprise. Without adventure there is no progress. No government administration can rightly take chances with taxpayers' money.

There is no better example of the practical incompetence of government to conduct business than the history of our railways. During the war the government found it necessary to operate the railways. That operation continued until after the war. In the year before being freed from government operation, they were not able to meet the demands for transportation. Eight years later we find them under private enterprise transporting 15 percent more goods and meeting every demand for service. Rates have been reduced by 15 percent and net earnings increased from less than 1 percent on their valuation to about 5 percent. Wages of employees have improved by 13 percent. The wages of railway employees are today 121 percent above prewar, while the wages of government employees are today only 65 percent above prewar. That should be a sufficient commentary upon the efficiency of government operation. . . .

Bureaucracy is ever desirous of spreading its influence and its power. You cannot extend the mastery of the government over the daily working life of a people without at the same time making it the master of the people's souls and thoughts. Every expansion of government in business means that government in order to protect itself from the political consequences of its errors and wrongs is driven irresistibly without peace to greater and greater control of the nation's press and platform. Free speech does not live many hours after free industry and free commerce die.

It is a false liberalism that interprets itself into the government operation of commercial business. Every step of bureaucratizing of the business of our country poisons the very roots of liberalism—that is, political equality, free speech, free assembly, free press, and equality of opportunity. It is the road not to more liberty, but to less liberty. Liberalism should be found not striving to spread bureaucracy but striving to set bounds to it. True liberalism seeks all legitimate freedom first in the confident belief that without such freedom the pursuit of all other blessings and benefits is vain. That belief is the foundation of all American progress, political as well as economic.

Liberalism is a force truly of the spirit, a force proceeding from the deep realization that economic freedom cannot be sacrificed if political freedom is to be preserved. Even if governmental conduct of business could give us more efficiency instead of less efficiency, the fundamental objection to it would remain unaltered and unabated. It would destroy political equality. It would increase rather than decrease abuse and corruption. It would stifle initiative and invention. It would undermine the development of leadership. It would cramp and cripple the mental and spiritual energies of our people. It would extinguish equality and opportunity. It would dry up the spirit of liberty and progress. For these reasons primarily it must be resisted. For 150 years liberalism has found its true spirit in the American system, not in the European systems.

I do not wish to be misunderstood in this statement. I am defining a general policy. It does not mean that our government is to part with one iota of its national resources without complete protection to the public interest. I have already stated that where the government is engaged in public works for purposes of flood control, of navigation, of irrigation, of scientific research or national defense, or in pioneering a new art, it will at times necessarily produce power or commodities as a by-product. But they must be a by-product of the major purpose, not the major purpose itself.

Nor do I wish to be misinterpreted as believing that the United States is a free-for-all and devil-take-the-hindmost. The very essence of equality of opportunity and of American individualism is that there shall be no domination by any group or combination in this republic, whether it be business or political. On the contrary, it demands economic justice. It is no system of *laissez faire*.

I feel deeply on this subject because during the war I had some practical experience with governmental operation and control. I have witnessed not only at home but abroad the many failures of government in business. I have seen its tyrannies, its injustices, its destructions of self-government, its undermining of the very instincts which carry our people forward to progress. I have witnessed the lack of advance, the lowered standards of living, the depressed spirits of people working under such a system. My objection is based not upon theory or upon a failure to recognize wrong or abuse, but I know the adoption of such methods would strike at the very roots of American life and would destroy the very basis of American progress.

Our people have the right to know whether we can continue to solve our great problems without abandonment of our American system. I know we can. We have demonstrated that our system is responsive enough to meet any new and intricate development in our economic and business life. We have demonstrated that we can meet any economic problem and still maintain our democracy as master in its own house, and that we can at the same time preserve equality of opportunity and individual freedom.

In the last fifty years we have discovered that mass production will produce articles for us at half the cost they required previously. We have seen the resultant growth of large units of production and distribution. This is big business. Many businesses must be bigger, for our tools are bigger, our country is bigger. We now build a single dynamo of 100,000 horsepower. Even fifteen years ago that would have been a big business all by itself. Yet today advance in production requires that we set ten of these units together in a row.

The American people from bitter experience have a rightful fear that great business units might be used to dominate our industrial life and by illegal and unethical practices destroy equality of opportunity.

Years ago the Republican administration established the principle that such evils could be corrected by regulation. It developed methods by which abuses could be prevented while the full value of industrial progress could be retained for the public. It insisted upon the principle that when great public utilities were clothed with the security of partial monopoly, whether it be railways, power plants, telephones, or what not, then there must be the fullest and most complete control of rates, services, and finances by government or local agencies. It declared that these businesses must be conducted with glass pockets.

As to our great manufacturing and distributing industries, the Republican Party insisted upon the enactment of laws that not only would maintain competition but would destroy conspiracies to destroy the smaller units or dominate and limit the equality of opportunity among our people.

One of the great problems of government is to determine to what extent the government shall regulate and control commerce and industry and how much it shall leave it alone. No system is perfect. We have had many abuses in the private conduct of business. That every good citizen resents. It is just as important that business keep out of government as that government keep out of business.

Nor am I setting up the contention that our institutions are perfect. No human ideal is ever perfectly attained, since humanity itself is not perfect.

The wisdom of our forefathers in their conception that progress can only be attained as the sum of the accomplishment of free individuals has been reinforced by all of the great leaders of the country since that day. Jackson, Lincoln, Cleveland, McKinley, Roosevelt, Wilson, and Coolidge have stood unalterably for these principles.

And what have been the results of our American system? Our country has become the land of opportunity to those born without inheritance, not merely because of the wealth of its resources and industry but because of this freedom of initiative and enterprise. Russia has natural resources equal to ours. Her people are equally industrious, but she has not had the blessings of 150 years of our form of government and of our social system.

By adherence to the principles of decentralized self-government, ordered liberty, equal opportunity, and freedom to the individual, our American experiment in human welfare has yielded a degree of well-being unparalleled in all the world. It has come nearer to the abolition of poverty, to the abolition of fear of want than humanity has ever reached before. Progress of the past seven years is the proof of it. This alone furnishes the answer to our opponents, who ask us to introduce destructive elements into the system by which this has been accomplished.

The Power of Confucian Capitalism 16

*Morishima Michio**

The economic disputes between Japan and the West are not merely problems of yen, cars, television sets, or tariff barriers. They are symptoms of basic social-philosophical conflicts. The West can no longer afford to ignore the Japanese outlook, particularly because Asian countries that follow Japan economically—such as Korea, Taiwan, Singapore, and Hong Kong—all have similar social philosophies.

The modern countries of Europe evolved in very different ways from Japan. Modern European political organizations were the product of clashes and compromise between feudal lords and the middle class; feudalism was abolished in Japan in 1868 not because the Japanese bourgeoisie demanded it but because it appeared that under feudalism the country would never become a great power and match the strength of the European powers. Compulsory education was instituted in Japan as early as 1872, not because the government recognized the significance of education for its own sake but because of the belief that the general level of education had to be raised to establish a great nation. Thus, to build a modern state, Japan adopted many Western systems despite the absence of conditions similar to those from which these systems had emerged in Europe.

Capitalism began in Japan in a unique way. When Japan began to build a modern State after the Meiji Revolution of 1867–68 there was no powerful bourgeoisie, so she introduced state capitalism and established factories with money raised by taxation or by issuing paper currency. The government soon fell into financial distress and had to sell most of its factories at low prices to retired government officials, or to private firms in which they were executives.

---

* Professor Morishima is currently affiliated with the London School of Economics. He was educated at Kyoto University before and after World War II. From *The Observer*, November, 1978.

These individuals suddenly became big capitalists. This is in contrast to the emergence of Western capitalists, who had to establish themselves by their own efforts, often in opposition to the state.

The very spirit of Japanese capitalism is different from that of Europe. Max Weber stressed that European capitalism was related to the Protestant ethic of asceticism. In the early years of Western capitalism neither the accumulation of capital (which Marx called "primitive accumulation") nor the propensity to invest (which Marx described in the famous line, "Accumulate, accumulate; that is Moses and the Prophets") would have been possible had Protestants not prevailed among capitalists. It would also have been impossible for Western capitalists to exploit workers had the latter not been sober and industrious and regarded work as a life purpose.

In Japan the two main religions, Buddhism and Shintoism, have had almost no influence on secular or economic conduct. This is one consequence of the educational policy of the Tokugawa Government before the Meiji period, which for more than two centuries supported and encouraged Confucianism. In Japan today Confucianism influences the everyday conduct of Buddhists and Shintoists and even Christians.

Confucianism, which the Japanese view as an ethic rather than a religion, holds the following virtues as most important: loyalty to the state or the emperor, filial piety, faith in friendship, and respect for elders. It is primarily concerned with the individual's relationship to various communities.

Confucianism discourages individualism. It is intellectual and rational in character, rejecting the mysticism and incantation common to other religions. The ability of the Japanese to assimilate Western technology and science with astonishing rapidity after the Meiji Revolution, was due at least in part to their education under Confucianism; Western rationalist thinking was not entirely foreign.

In Confucian political thought, those who play the most important roles in society are the bureaucrats. Under that philosophy, the feudal age of Tokugawa was an era of bureaucratic rule during which a samurai was a civil as well as military officer. The Meiji Government was an advanced modern bureaucracy from the outset.

Though they compete to be selected, once they are chosen Japanese bureaucrats do not compete with one another, thanks to the system of lifelong employment and seniority which is an outgrowth of Confucianism. Japanese companies however, do compete keenly. Workers and staff are soldiers and officers in this battle, fighting not for themselves but for their firms.

An important element in the development of the modern Japanese economy was the country's almost total involvement in war from 1931 to 1945. When World War II ended, most men under forty had no working background except as soldiers. With no managerial experience, they operated firms the way they had commanded platoons. The workers, who as soldiers had existed precariously between life and death, found monotonous factory work by no means unbearable. Loyalty to firms took the place of wartime loyalty to the state. In this way, the collectivist character of Confucian capitalism was strengthened.

One may console oneself with the belief that Japan will become Westernized because of her economic achievements. But no one really knows what course an economically mature Confucian capitalist country will take.

The Work Ethic and How It Grew 17

Frank Gibney*

In 1868, with the fleets of European powers at their ports demanding
admittance and free trade for their manufactures, samurai of the Japanese lower nobility, led by the two powerful southern clans of Satsuma
and Choshu, united to depose the last of the Tokugawa shoguns and
restore the emperor, in the extraordinary self-modernization of the
Meiji Restoration. The immediate purpose of Japan's Meiji modernization was defensive. The Japanese had to save themselves from the
semicolonial status to which the Western powers, by virtue of their
superior armament and industrial abilities, were reducing China. But
there were far wider issues involved. During the two hundred fifty
years of the Tokugawa shogunate, the Japanese had lived in guarded
seclusion from the outside world. Within their islands, backward as
they were in technical matters, the Japanese had developed a bustling,
energetic, and venturesome small business and trading society, based
on the trading houses and merchant bankers of Osaka, Tokyo, and
Kyoto. Chafing under the rule of the shogunate, some of the clan
domains, notably Satsuma and Choshu, had built up not only commercial networks of their own but also small fledgling industries,
started with forbidden imports from the West. It was clear to the young
Meiji reformers that Japan must now build its own steel mills and
textile factories on a nationwide scale so that there would be a business
and industrial foundation for the *fukoku kyohei* (a prosperous country
and a strong army) ideals of the Restoration.

The Meiji officials were for the most part reformers, not revolu-
tionaries. They had no wish to disrupt the fabric of Japanese society.

---

* Frank Gibney is an American journalist and businessman who has lived and worked in Japan,
and was responsible for the rapid expansion and diversification of Encyclopaedia Britannica in
that country. From *Miracle by Design: The Real Reasons behind Japan's Economic Success,* by Frank
Gibney (New York: Times Books, 1982).

They much preferred to build on what they already had. They abolished political feudalism in favor of national loyalty to the emperor. But the basic Confucian hierarchies of the Tokugawa world remained in fact, if not in law. So did the loyalties that went with them. Commoners no longer needed think of themselves as second-class citizens in the rigid relationships. It was the businessman's turn to manage new modern mills and trading companies as a full partner in the country's progress toward Civilization and Enlightenment, to quote another Meiji slogan. Yet naturally enough, when the Meiji people started the foundations of modern enterprise, they relied for their organization on the old apprenticeship systems of the Tokugawa merchants. . . .

Work was seen as service of long commitment, "not purely an economic act but a spiritual and moral experience," as Yamamoto noted in his book. The tradition-hallowed ranks of apprentice, assistant clerk, clerk, and head clerk (*detchi, tedai, banto, dobanto*) of the old Osaka trading houses (one of them, the House of Mitsui, had been founded in 1637) were translated into modern terms that have remained in Japanese business to this day. Unlike Europe, where the Industrial Revolution smashed feudal bonds and obediences (often in favor of more onerous varieties of serfdom), in Japan a semifeudal family system of doing business was simply transplanted into a modern capitalist society. The thinking about the seniority system and lifetime employment had its origins in (the 18th century Confucian, Ishida) Baigan's day, as did the idea of the clerk going into business for himself as a junior or branch house of the parent firm. The ancient system of main family (*honke*) and branch family (*bunke*) business, as formalized by the Tokugawa, are what lie behind the modern Japanese corporation's rationale for establishing subsidiaries. So is the idea of the company as a kind of large family organization, a new territorial group but nonetheless one with its own family consciousness, to be entered by a new company person, with appropriate rites and examinations, less in the manner of a worker joining a functional organization than that of a new member joining a lifetime club.

True to Baigan's philosophy, the idea of service to the community and "the empire" was ingrained in the new company structure. This was all the more necessary since most entrepreneurs of the big new businesses came from the samurai class, the same two-sworded gentry who had until the mid-1800s thought of the trader as a low species of humanity and were themselves unwilling to handle money.

Other unique features of Japanese capitalism began to surface at this time. Since no modern industry existed, the government itself had to start up the new factories and mills, then sell them off to private entrepreneurs or investors in the new joint-stock companies. So emerged the close cooperative relationship between government and business. Almost no capital was available for starting major modern industries. Hence the government had to set up a national taxation system, then establish a national bank, the Bank of Japan, to supply money and control it, through the new city banks. The heavy dependence of Japanese companies on bank financing and their high leverage policies started almost with their origins. Like the ties of development and cooperation between government and business, these were part of a new capitalist tradition, developing from necessity as much as invention.

The administrative bureaucracy of the Meiji government was staffed by the samurai class. Most of them had gained valuable administrative experience working as clan or shogunate officials. Journalists and educators also came from this class. So did many entrepreneurs of the new state businesses, who received their working capital in the form of government subsidies or concessions. Iwasaki Yataro, the founder of the Mitsubishi group, was a young samurai from the southern clan of Tosa when the Restoration took place. He got his start in 1874, when the government gave him thirteen ships to ferry troops in the Formosan expedition. Sixteen years later the government sold off its Nagasaki shipyards to Mitsubishi and in the same year some large tracts of land in Tokyo not far from the Imperial Palace, the beginnings of Mitsubishi's vast real estate empire. Similarly, Furukawa Ichibei, a young merchant from Kyoto, received a government charter in 1877 to develop the copper mines at Ashio. He parlayed this original investment into a network of electric companies, cable companies, light metal companies, and others, one of which ultimately became Fujitsu, the modern computer giant.

One reason that samurai took over some of the big new companies was that the average merchant, especially if he came from the old trading houses, was generally cautious about going into new enterprises. The House of Mitsui, which had helped finance the emperor's forces, was an outstanding exception. Others, like the equally prestigious House of Ono, could not meet the new challenges. Ono went bankrupt shortly after the Restoration, thanks to an overambitious investment in a new silk-reeling mill. Many of the old-fashioned merchants expanded only modestly, content either to continue manufactures of traditional Japanese materials or to serve as subcontractors for the big new government-subsidized companies. Here is the origin of the peculiar dual structure in Japanese business—the parallel existence of big business on one track and small or medium-sized businesses on another, with greatly reduced wage levels and job security. This has continued into our day.

Nonetheless, when the new large enterprises took shape, they were almost uniformly modeled on the old family merchant houses of Tokugawa days. There were four major *zaibatsu* (money clique) enterprises—Mitsui, Mitsubishi, Sumitomo, and Yasuda—conglomerates with interests in almost every branch of industry. Mitsui's prewar interests, for example, included mining, shipping, oil, cement, automobiles (Toyota was originally a Mitsui company), chemicals, precision machinery, textiles, flour, real estate, and of course, at the center of the group's activities, the Mitsui Bank. There were about sixteen other smaller *zaibatsu* organisms, organized in more specialized areas, like Furukawa, Okura, or Asano. All of them were controlled by tight family organizations at the top. Through holding companies and interlocking directorates (a control device beloved by Japanese businessmen to this day), smaller subsidiaries were knit into the organization. Close to government and themselves governed by ponderous hierarchies, these Japanese-style conglomerates were nonetheless a far cry from the later American variety that bought and sold companies for quick profit. As with the Tokugawa protocapitalists, they were territorialists who habitually put their money into capital improvement and expansion. In *The Economic Development of Japan* the late William Lockwood summarized their activities:

> They performed an essential function in large-scale enterprise which could otherwise have been performed only by the state and not necessarily with greater public benefit. If they reaped fabulous gains, as they did, they continued to plough back the larger share in entrepreneurial investment in new and expanding activity.

Baigan would not have disowned them.

Most of the Meiji industrialists were sadly wanting, however, in one important respect: fair treatment of their employees. Workers in that day were poorly paid and had virtually no security. Indeed the workplaces of industrializing Japan were local variations of the "dark satanic mills" that first sprang up in Europe during the Industrial Revolution. Not until the 1920s were halfway decent labor laws enacted, which gave at least some safeguards against the exploitation of women and children.

While taking advantage of the loyalties of the Japanese worker, the new Meiji capitalists did not reciprocate. The full employment idea, which had been part of the Tokugawa trading houses, was thrown out with industrialization. It was not brought back until the years after World War I, when skilled labor shortages made Japanese employers realize that it was better economics to keep a competent worker than to let him go and try to hire another. Unlike their American and European colleagues, they could not count on a constant flow of immigrants or a large reserve of fairly skilled workers. Only grudgingly did Japanese businessmen move toward the full employment policy of which they boast today. Even then, only the big *zaibatsu* enterprises could afford to do so. The films of the twenties and thirties are full of young "salary men" from small companies being fired out of hand by a screaming boss with a clipped Charlie Chaplin mustache, yelling *"kubi do"* ("You're fired"). It took the U.S. Occupation to give Japanese workers the guarantees of working standards and bargaining rights, which in the end profited and strengthened both sides.

Small Is Beautiful 18

E. F. Schumacher

Buddhist Economics

"Right Livelihood" is one of the requirements of the Buddha's Noble Eightfold Path. It is clear, therefore, that there must be such a thing as Buddhist economics.

Buddhist countries have often stated that they wish to remain faithful to their heritage. So Burma: "The New Burma sees no conflict between religious values and economic progress. Spiritual health and material well-being are not enemies: they are natural allies." Or: "We can blend successfully the religious and spiritual values of our heritage with the benefits of modern technology." Or: "We Burmans have a sacred duty to conform both our dreams and our acts to our faith. This we shall ever do."

All the same, such countries invariably assume that they can model their economic development plans in accordance with modern economics, and they call upon modern economists from so-called advanced countries to advise them, to formulate the policies to be pursued, and to construct the grand design for development, the Five-Year Plan or whatever it may be called. No one seems to think that a Buddhist way of life would call for Buddhist economics, just as the modern materialist way of life has brought forth modern economics.

Economists themselves, like most specialists, normally suffer from a kind of metaphysical blindness, assuming that theirs is a science of absolute and invariable truths, without any presuppositions. Some go as far as to claim that economic laws are as free from "metaphysics" or "values" as the law of gravitation. We need not, however, get involved in arguments of methodology. Instead, let us take some fundamentals and see what they look like when viewed by a modern economist and a Buddhist economist.

There is universal agreement that a fundamental source of wealth is human labour. Now, the modern economist has been brought up to consider "labour" or work as little more than a necessary evil. From the point of view of the employer, it is in any case simply an item of cost, to be reduced to a minimum if it cannot be eliminated altogether, say, by automation. From the point of view of the workman, it is a "disutility"; to work is to make a sacrifice of one's leisure and comfort, and wages are a kind of compensation for the sacrifice. Hence the ideal from the point of view of the employer is to have output without employees, and the ideal from the point of view of the employee is to have income without employment.

The consequences of these attitudes both in theory and in practise are, of course, extremely far-reaching. If the ideal with regard to work is to get rid of it, every method that "reduces the work load" is a good thing. The most potent method, short of automation, is the so-called "division of labour" and the classical example is the pin factory eulogised in Adam Smith's *Wealth of Nations*. Here it is not a matter of ordinary specialisation, which mankind has practised from time immemorial, but of dividing up every complete process of production into minute parts, so that the final product can be produced at great speed without anyone having had to contribute more than a totally insignificant and, in most cases, unskilled movement of his limbs.

The Buddhist point of view takes the function of work to be at least threefold: to give a man a chance to utilise and develop his faculties; to enable him to overcome his ego-centredness by joining with other people in a common task; and to bring forth the goods and services needed for a becoming existence. Again, the consequences that flow from this view are endless. To organise work in such a manner that it becomes meaningless, boring, stultifying, or nerve-racking for the worker would be little short of criminal; it would indicate a greater concern with goods than with people, an evil lack of compassion and a soul-destroying degree of attachment to the most primitive side of this worldly existence. Equally, to strive for leisure as an alternative to work would be considered a complete misunderstanding of one of the basic truths of human existence, namely that work and leisure are complementary parts of the same living process and cannot be separated without destroying the joy of work and the bliss of leisure.

From the Buddhist point of view, there are therefore two types of mechanisation which must be clearly distinguished: one that enhances a man's skill and power and one that turns the work of man over to a mechanical slave, leaving man in a position of having to serve the slave. How to tell the one from the other? "The craftsman himself," says Ananda Coomaraswamy, a man equally competent to talk about the modern West as the ancient East, "can always, if allowed to, draw the delicate distinction between the machine and the tool. The carpet loom is a tool, a contrivance for holding warp threads at a stretch for the pile to be woven around them by the craftsmen's fingers; but the power loom is a machine, and its significance as a destroyer of culture lies in the fact that it does the essentially human part of the work." It is clear, therefore, that Buddhist economics must be very different from the economics of modern materialism, since the Buddhist sees the essence of civilisation not in a multiplication of wants but in the purification of human character. Character, at the same time, is formed primarily by a man's work. And work, properly conducted in conditions of human dignity and freedom, blesses those who do it and equally their products. The Indian philosopher and economist, J. C. Kumarappa sums the matter up as follows:

> If the nature of the work is properly appreciated and applied, it will stand in the same relation to the higher faculties as food is to the physical body. It nourishes and enlivens the higher man and urges him to produce the best he is capable of. It directs his free will along the proper course and disciplines the animal in him into progressive channels. It furnishes an excellent background for man to display his scale of values and develop his personality.

If a man has no chance of obtaining work he is in a desperate position, not simply because he lacks an income but because he lacks this nourishing and enlivening factor of disciplined work which nothing can replace. A modern economist may engage in highly sophisticated calculations on whether full employment "pays" or whether it might be more "economic" to run an economy at less than full employment so as to ensure a greater mobility of labour, a better stability of wages, and so forth. His fundamental criterion of success is simply the total quantity of goods produced during a given period of time. "If the marginal urgency of goods is low," says Professor Galbraith in *The Affluent Society,* "then so is the urgency of employing the last man or the last million men in the labour force." And again: "If . . . we can afford some unemployment in the interest of stability—a proposition, incidentally, of impeccably conservative antecedents—then we can afford to give those who are unemployed the goods that enable them to sustain their accustomed standard of living."

From a Buddhist point of view, this is standing the truth on its head by considering goods as more important than people and consumption as more important than creative activity. It means shifting the emphasis from the worker to the product of work, that is, from the human to the subhuman, a surrender to the forces of evil. The very start of Buddhist economic planning would be a planning for full employment, and the primary purpose of this would in fact be employment for everyone who needs an "outside" job: it would not be the maximisation of employment nor the maximisation of production. Women, on the whole, do not need an "outside" job, and the large-scale employment of women in offices or factories would be considered a sign of serious economic failure. In particular, to let mothers of young children work in factories while the children run wild would be as uneconomic in the eyes of a Buddhist economist as the employment of a skilled worker as a soldier in the eyes of a modern economist.

While the materialist is mainly interested in goods, the Buddhist is mainly interested in liberation. But Buddhism is "The Middle Way" and therefore in no way antagonistic to physical well-being. It is not wealth that stands in the way of liberation but the attachment to wealth; not the enjoyment of pleasurable things but the craving for them. The keynote of Buddhist economics, therefore, is simplicity and nonviolence. From an economist's point of view, the marvel of the Buddhist way of life is the utter rationality of its pattern—amazingly small means leading to extraordinarily satisfactory results.

For the modern economist this is very difficult to understand. He is used to measuring the "standard of living" by the amount of annual consumption, assuming all the time that a man who consumes more is "better off" than a man who consumes less. A Buddhist economist would consider this approach excessively irrational: since consumption is merely a means to human well-being, the aim should be to obtain the maximum of well-being with the minimum of consumption. Thus, if the purpose of clothing is a certain amount of temperature comfort and an attractive appearance, the task is to attain this purpose with the smallest possible effort, that is, with the smallest annual destruction of cloth and with the help of designs that involve the smallest possible input of toil. The less toil there is, the more time and strength is left for artistic creativity. It would be highly uneconomic, for instance, to go in for complicated tailoring, like the modern West, when a much more beautiful effect can be achieved by the skilful draping of uncut material. It would be the height of folly to make material so that it should wear out quickly and the height of barbarity to make anything ugly, shabby or mean. What has just been said about clothing applies equally to all other human requirements. The ownership and the consumption of goods is a means to an end, and Buddhist economics is the systematic study of how to attain given ends with the minimum means.

Modern economics, on the other hand, considers consumption to be the sole end and purpose of all economic activity, taking the factors of production—land, labour, and capital—as the means. The former, in short, tries to maximise human satisfactions by the optimal pattern of consumption, while the latter tries to maximise consumption by the optimal pattern of productive effort. It is easy to see that the effort needed to sustain a way of life which seeks to attain the optimal pattern of consumption is likely to be much smaller than the effort needed to sustain a drive for maximum consumption. We need not be surprised, therefore, that the pressure and strain of living is very much less in, say, Burma than it is in the United States, in spite of the fact that the amount of labour-saving machinery used in the former country is only a minute fraction of the amount used in the latter.

Simplicity and nonviolence are obviously closely related. The optimal pattern of consumption, producing a high degree of human satisfaction by means of a relatively low rate of consumption, allows people to live without great pressure and strain and to fulfil the primary injunction of Buddhist teaching: "Cease to do evil; try to do good." As physical resources are everywhere limited, people satisfying their needs by means of a modest use of resources are obviously less likely to be at each other's throats than people depending upon a high rate of use. Equally, people who live in highly self-sufficient local communities are less likely to get involved in large-scale violence than people whose existence depends upon worldwide systems of trade.

From the point of view of Buddhist economics, therefore, production from local resources for local needs is the most rational way of economic life, while dependence on imports from afar and the consequent need to produce for export to unknown and distant peoples is highly uneconomic and justifiable only in exceptional cases and on a small scale. Just as the modern economist would admit that a high rate of consumption of transport services between a man's home and his place of work signifies a misfortune and not a high standard of life, so the Buddhist economist would hold that to satisfy human wants from faraway sources rather than from sources nearby signifies failure rather than success. The former tends to take statistics showing an increase in the number of ton/miles per head of the population carried by a country's transport system as proof of economic progress, while to the latter—the Buddhist economist—the same statistics would indicate a highly undesirable deterioration in the *pattern* of consumption.

Another striking difference between modern economics and Buddhist economics arises over the use of natural resources. Bertrand de Jouvenel, the eminent French political philosopher, has characterised "Western man" in words which may be taken as a fair description of the modern economist:

> He tends to count nothing as an expenditure, other than human effort;
> he does not seem to mind how much mineral matter he wastes and, far
> worse, how much living matter he destroys. He does not seem to realise at

all that human life is a dependent part of an ecosystem of many different forms of life. As the world is ruled from towns where men are cut off from any form of life other than human, the feeling of belonging to an ecosystem is not revived. This results in a harsh and improvident treatment of things upon which we ultimately depend, such as water and trees.

The teaching of the Buddha, on the other hand, enjoins a reverent and nonviolent attitude not only to all sentient beings but also, with great emphasis, to trees. Every follower of the Buddha ought to plant a tree every few years and look after it until it is safely established, and the Buddhist economist can demonstrate without difficulty that the universal observation of this rule would result in a high rate of genuine economic development independent of any foreign aid. Much of the economic decay of southeast Asia (as of many other parts of the world) is undoubtedly due to a heedless and shameful neglect of trees.

Modern economics does not distinguish between renewable and nonrenewable materials, as its very method is to equalise and quantify everything by means of a money price. Thus, taking various alternative fuels, like coal, oil, wood, or water-power: the only difference between them recognised by modern economics is relative cost per equivalent unit. The cheapest is automatically the one to be preferred, as to do otherwise would be irrational and "uneconomic." From a Buddhist point of view, of course, this will not do; the essential difference between nonrenewable fuels like coal and oil on the one hand and renewable fuels like wood and water-power on the other cannot be simply overlooked. Nonrenewable goods must be used only if they are indispensable, and then only with the greatest care and the most meticulous concern for conservation. To use them heedlessly or extravagantly is an act of violence, and while complete nonviolence may not be attainable on this earth, there is nonetheless an ineluctable duty on man to aim at the ideal of nonviolence in all he does.

Just as a modern European economist would not consider it a great economic achievement if all European art treasures were sold to America at attractive prices, so the Buddhist economist would insist that a population basing its economic life on nonrenewable fuels is living parasitically, on capital instead of income. Such a way of life could have no permanence and could therefore be justified only as a purely temporary expedient. As the world's resources of nonrenewable fuels—coal, oil and natural gas—are exceedingly unevenly distributed over the globe and undoubtedly limited in quantity, it is clear that their exploitation at an ever-increasing rate is an act of violence against nature which must almost inevitably lead to violence between men.

This fact alone might give food for thought even to those people in Buddhist countries who care nothing for the religious and spiritual values of their heritage and ardently desire to embrace the materialism of modern economics at the fastest possible speed. Before they dismiss Buddhist economics as nothing better than a nostalgic dream, they might wish to consider whether the path of economic development outlined by modern economics is likely to lead them to places where they really want to be. Towards the end of his courageous book *The Challenge of Man's Future,* Professor Harrison Brown of the California Institute of Technology gives the following appraisal:

> Thus we see that, just as industrial society is fundamentally unstable and subject to reversion to agrarian existence, so within it the conditions which offer individual freedom are unstable in their ability to avoid the conditions which impose rigid organisation and totalitarian control. Indeed, when we examine all of the foreseeable difficulties which threaten the survival of industrial civilisation, it is difficult to see how the achievement of stability and the maintenance of individual liberty can be made compatible.

Even if this were dismissed as a long-term view there is the immediate question of whether "modernisation," as currently practised without regard to religious and spiritual values, is actually producing agreeable results. As far as the masses are concerned, the results appear to be disastrous—a collapse of the rural economy, a rising tide of unemployment in town and country, and the growth of a city proletariat without nourishment for either body or soul.

It is in the light of both immediate experience and long-term prospects that the study of Buddhist economics could be recommended even to those who believe that economic growth is more important than any spiritual or religious values. For it is not a question of choosing between "modern growth" and "traditional stagnation." It is a question of finding the right path of development, the Middle Way between materialist heedlessness and traditionalist immobility, in short, of finding "Right Livelihood."

The Malcolm Baldrige Program What It's About— Where It Fits and Approaches for Its Use

6

Richard J. Pierce

Quality Executive, Aerospace Group (Ret.)

General Electric Corporation

INTRODUCTION

Richard Pierce informs us that the Malcolm Baldrige guidelines fit well within the framework of broader guidelines to build a foundation for Total Quality. Guidelines for the foundation are included in all preceding parts of this book
Pierce focuses on the Malcolm Baldrige Program and tells:

- What the program is about
- How it fits
- Strategic Quality Planning approaches for its use

FOREWORD

After 30 years, American business leaders have been given a powerful new weapon for competing against foreign companies in international markets, and against other American companies in domestic markets. It is the Malcolm Baldrige guidelines that describe the latest and most comprehensive version of Total Quality.

The guidelines are a powerful weapon because they have been developed over a period of ten years by an extraordinary consortium of the most experienced and knowledgeable leaders involved in Total Quality. President Reagan, then-Vice-President Bush, and Secretary of Commerce Baldrige were concerned about our nation's ability to compete in quality and productivity. They provided leadership, sustained by President Bush and Secretary of Commerce Mosbacher, to create the consortium. It included leaders of companies who have installed earlier versions of Total Quality, internationally renouned American quality experts, University professors, officials from professional societies, and unions coordinated by Department of Commerce officials. The consortium did not underestimate the challenge.

A smart-thinking business leader will seek a perspective about where the Malcolm Baldrige guidelines fit within a larger framework of guidelines for Total Quality. The leader will learn that some broader guidelines need attention before applying the Malcolm Baldrige guidelines.

A foundation must be built. Attitudes, behavior, and management style must be changed. Knowledge must be acquired about why American goods declined in quality and productivity rates fell, and how foreign nations overtook us. This includes recognizing the vital advantages that foreign companies have structured, and realizing that they must be matched in American companies. Nearly all foreign companies have structured company-wide Total Quality to replace Department Quality Control, escalated Total Quality leadership to the President or Chief Executive Officer, and operate on long-range philosophies instead of annual business goals. The foundation must include visions of short- and, particularly, long-range missions, objectives, and values for without them there can be no planning.

Knowledge is also needed about the American heritage in which philosophers, business leaders and statesmen employed capitalism to create the greatest American national economy the world has known. Of importance, too, is knowledge of recent business leaders' successful efforts to build individual versions of foundations and Total Quality at their companies.

Leaders who have built a solid foundation and then established the Malcolm Baldrige version of Total Quality have developed confidence in the enduring nature of their efforts and, especially, in their ability to compete. All employees are invigorated and strengthened by a sense of belonging, and by an environment of teamwork within the company and with suppliers. They know they have greater respect from customers and that their market share is increasing.

Many company leaders are giving insufficient attention to a foundation and, too soon, assign teams to fulfill the seven primary criteria of the Malcolm Baldrige guidelines. This approach creates a temporary euphoria within the company, eventually followed by loss of creditability by employees, disenchantment by managers, and orders by the Chief Executive Officer to cancel and return to square one.

WHAT THE MALCOLM BALDRIGE PROGRAM IS ABOUT

Curt W. Reimann, the Director of The Malcolm Baldrige Program, in the Department of Commerce, describes the growing concern about competitiveness. The history, the organization, and outlines are featured in his speech. "The Malcolm Baldrige National Quality Award." (See Appendix D.) Reimann continually solicits improvements to the Program from Examiners and many others in the consortium, and he receives counsel from the Chairman of the Board of Overseers. These are incorporated in "Annual Application Guidelines, Malcolm Baldrige National Quality Award." You can obtain applications from the Malcolm Baldrige Program Office or from the American Society for Quality Control.

Key elements of the Program are described employing illustrations from the latest Application Guidelines, other Malcolm Baldrige material, and some insights and observations from an Examiner.

Public Law 100–107, The Quality Improvement Act, was enacted in 1987 and is based on the awareness of the realities of the changing global marketplace, the importance quality has in our competitiveness, and the effect of quality on America's standard of living.

Its purposes include:

• Promoting quality awareness and practices in U.S. businesses

• Recognizing quality achievements of U.S. companies

• Publicize successful strategies and programs

Another purpose, often not understood, is to encourage competition between American companies in domestic marketplaces. The rationale is that such competition raises the level of quality and productivity throughout America, and stimulates the national economy. The purpose is not to provide "how to" guides, nor is it a means for Examiners to "feedback" prescriptions for improving quality or productivity.

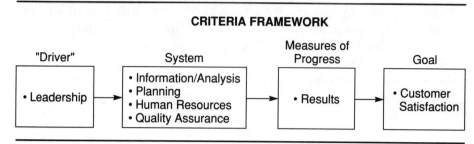

FIGURE 1

There are currently three categories of awards:

- Manufacturing Companies (including Agriculture, Mining, and Construction)

- Service Companies

- Small Business (Fewer than 500 employees is one current definition)

Two awards per category are authorized, if warranted.

It is noteworthy that communication about the Malcolm Baldrige Program is easier with large Fortune 500 companies then with medium- and small-size businesses, and with service business. Attention is being given to this condition.

The guidelines provide the criteria for applicants to apply for the National Quality Award. They are also intended for companies that are not seeking the Award, but are using the criteria as a standard to improve their quality and productivity.

Only communication between a company top official and the Director or Deputy Director of the Malcolm Baldrige Program can determine eligibility for the Award.

The heart of the Program is the criteria framework given in Figure 1. The intent is that the seven primary criteria that form the framework will be permanent. There are currently 32 examination items and 99 additional "areas to be addressed" for evaluating the criteria. Some changes resulting from suggested improvements are presented in the Annual Guidelines.

Figure 2, taken from the Examiner's Scorebook, defines the seven primary criteria, the thirty-three examination items, and areas to be addressed. Further, it shows the weighting given each item, the basis for evaluation and scoring, and provisions for scoring individual items, scoring for each criteria, and for total scores.

Examiner Name ——————————————————————————————

Applicant Name ————————————————— Applicant Number ——————— **2**

SUMMARY OF EXAMINATION ITEMS	Total Points Possible	Percent Score 0-100% (10% units)	Score (A x B)
	A	**B**	**C**
1.0 LEADERSHIP 100 POSSIBLE POINTS			
1.1 Senior Executive Leadership	30	_____%	_____
1.2 Quality Values	20	_____%	_____
1.3 Management for Quality	30	_____%	_____
1.4 Public Responsibility	20	_____%	_____
Category Total	**100** SUM A		SUM C
2.0 INFORMATION AND ANALYSIS 60 POSSIBLE POINTS			
2.1 Scope and Management of Quality Data and Information	35	_____%	_____
2.2 Analysis of Quality Data and Information	25	_____%	_____
Category Total	**60** SUM A		SUM C
3.0 STRATEGIC QUALITY PLANNING 90 POSSIBLE POINTS			
3.1 Strategic Quality Planning Process	40	_____%	_____
3.2 Quality Leadership Indicators in Planning	25	_____%	_____
3.3 Quality Priorities	25	_____%	_____
Category Total	**90** SUM A		SUM C
4.0 HUMAN RESOURCE UTILIZATION 150 POSSIBLE POINTS			
4.1 Human Resource Management	30	_____%	_____
4.2 Employee Involvement	40	_____%	_____
4.3 Quality Education and Training	40	_____%	_____
4.4 Employee Recognition and Performance Measurement	20	_____%	_____
4.5 Employee Well-Being and Morale	20	_____%	_____
Category Total	**150** SUM A		SUM C
5.0 QUALITY ASSURANCE OF PRODUCTS AND SERVICES 150 POSSIBLE POINTS			
5.1 Design and Introduction of Quality Products and Services	30	_____%	_____
5.2 Process and Quality Control	25	_____%	_____
5.3 Continuous Improvement of Processes, Products, and Services	25	_____%	_____
5.4 Quality Assessment	15	_____%	_____
5.5 Documentation	10	_____%	_____
5.6 Quality Assurance, Quality Assessment and Quality Improvement of Support Services and Business Processes	25	_____%	_____
5.7 Quality Assurance, Quality Assessment and Quality Improvement of Suppliers	20	_____%	_____
Category Total	**150** SUM A		SUM C

FIGURE 2

Examiner Name ————————————————————————————
Applicant Name ————————————————— Applicant Number ——————— **2**

SUMMARY OF EXAMINATION ITEMS	Total Points Possible A	Percent Score 0-100% (10% units) B	Score (A x B) C
6.0 QUALITY RESULTS 150 POSSIBLE POINTS			
6.1 Quality of Products and Services	50	——— %	———
6.2 Comparison of Quality Results	35	——— %	———
6.3 Business Process, Operational and Support Service Quality Improvement	35	——— %	———
6.4 Supplier Quality Improvement	30	——— %	———
Category Total	**150** SUM A		SUM C
7.0 CUSTOMER SATISFACTION 300 POSSIBLE POINTS			
7.1 Knowledge of Customer Requirements and Expectations	50	——— %	———
7.2 Customer Relationship Management	30	——— %	———
7.3 Customer Service Standards	20	——— %	———
7.4 Commitment to Customers	20	——— %	———
7.5 Complaint Resolution for Quality Improvement	30	——— %	———
7.6 Customer Satisfaction Determination	50	——— %	———
7.7 Customer Satisfaction Results	50	——— %	———
7.8 Customer Satisfaction Comparison	50	——— %	———
Category Total	**300** SUM A		SUM C
GRAND TOTAL (D)	**1000**		D

For Supplemental Reports Only

	Total Score	x	Percent Sales	=	
Basic Report					
Supplemental Report 1	———	x	———	=	———
Supplemental Report 2	———	x	———	=	———
Supplemental Report 3	———	x	———	=	———
Supplemental Report 4	———	x	———	=	———
Supplemental Report 5	———	x	———	=	———
			Final Score		———

FIGURE 2, CONTINUED

The object of the evaluation and scoring processes is to determine the strengths of the company for meeting each examination item, and the areas that need improvement to meet the criteria. Judgement of the score awarded for each item is based on these findings. The figures show provisions for such findings.

Three evaluation dimensions are given for use in determining strengths and areas for improvement. They are: Approach, Deployment, and Results. Figure 3 describes the scoring criteria used to evaluate adherence to the three dimensions.

It is important to emphasize the weighting. The seven primary criteria are listed below in the order of the possible points they can contribute to the score:

FIGURE 3

Criteria	Possible Points
Customer Satisfaction	300
Human Resource Utilization	150
Quality Results	140
Quality Assurance of Products & Services	180
Leadership	100
Information & Analysis	60
Strategic Quality Planning	70

A benefit of applying for the award is that all applicants receive a feedback report that is a consensus of several examiners and also a judge, if a company's submission warrants a site visit.

A benefit of winning the Award is promotion of the company by the Department of Commerce. The applicant must agree to publicizing its strategy and methods for winning, except for the company's sensitive information.

A benefit to America's national economy and to American businesses is attainment of eminent competitive positions by employing the rigorous requirements of the Malcolm Baldrige Program.

WHERE THE MALCOLM BALDRIGE PROGRAM FITS

Let us examine in greater detail the fit between the Malcolm Baldrige Program and the foundation. The Program is part of a culture for American business that must be built upon the foundation.

There are explicit, though sometimes subtle, assumptions of the existence of a strong foundation in the Malcolm Baldrige criteria and three evaluation dimensions. Examples of assumptions and inferences of the relationships between the Program and the foundation are:

> The criteria for leadership by top and senior officials does not require that leadership for Total Quality be elevated to the CEO. Yet it is assumed. The expectations of leadership by and involvement of, senior officials makes changes to company-wide quality obvious, and transcends the old concept of Department Quality Control. The expectations are reinforced by the evaluation dimension of deployment. It is clear a foundation must escalate leadership of company-wide Total Quality to the CEO. Further, this leadership cannot be effected by "approval" of a

proposal, nor can it be delegated to the middle for providing leadership to the bottom. The CEO must provide strong and continuous personal involvement.

The essence of Total Quality is performance of people. Fulfilling the criteria for Human Resource Utilization is dependent upon the attitudes, behavior and participative style of management of the upper levels of the company. The foundation prescribes that changes must be made to create the right attitudes, behavior, and style before applying the Malcolm Baldrige guidelines. This cannot be scheduled easily, and patience is required to take whatever time is needed to effect the changes.

The criteria for Strategic Quality Planning and integration with Strategic Business Planning is dependent upon the place of Total Quality in the business, with visions of the company's short-, and particularly long-, range mission, objectives, and values of the company. The foundation establishes Total Quality as a primary instrument for competition for the company. It also develops the visions.

The Malcolm Baldrige Program guidelines provide systems for Total Quality. The Quality Control System has always provided the means for unifying the many elements of Quality Control, and identified external and internal customers. With the Program assumption of company-wide Total Quality, the need and the scope of a Quality System is increased. The foundation must develop the system.

The fit of the Malcolm Baldrige Program with the foundation is excellent. A solid foundation and the rigorous Malcolm Baldrige Program provide a culture for American business that can assure eminent competitive positions.

APPROACHES FOR USE OF THE MALCOLM BALDRIGE PROGRAM

The Malcolm Baldrige Program is a powerful weapon, but competitiveness is determined by how the weapon is used. The third primary criterion of the Program is concerned with Strategic Quality Planning and its integration with Strategic Business Planning. They provide the means for employing the weapon. However, some approaches achieve objectives, while other approaches do not.

Much has been written over the past two decades about Strategic Business Planning, but there is a paucity of information about Strategic Quality Planning. Examination of many submissions for the National Quality Award reveals a widespread need for more information about both. I will provide some definitions and insights, then proceed to describe approaches for using Strategic Quality Planning and integrating it into Strategic Business Planning.

Professor William F. Glueck, in his book "Business Policy and Strategic Management" acknowledges the role of the General Electric Company, ie: "- credit the General Electric Company with pioneering the rudiments of the concept "Strategic Business Planning" more than a decade ago." Reginald Jones was installed as President and was mandated to establish Strategic Business Planning throughout the company. Less well known is that he, with his Director for Quality, A. V. Feiganbaum, also created Strategic Quality Planning.

In the Aerospace Industries, the CEO of a major weapons acquisition is the Program Manager, with all the resources of a CEO and all responsibilities and accountabilities. As Program Manager of the first three generations of ReEntry Vehicles for Inter Continental Ballistic Missiles at General Electric, I was trained and charged with preparing the Strategic Business Plans. Later, as an Aerospace Group Quality Executive operating under the direction of, and with training from, A. V. Feigenbaum, I was charged with preparing Strategic Quality Plans and participating in the integration of these plans with Strategic Business Plans. I draw on this experience and the knowledge of more recent experts like Professor Glueck.

It is obvious that the broad objectives of business planning and quality planning are the same. The Strategic Quality Plan is a primary instrument for competitiveness and is a part of the Strategic Business Plan. Some definitions and insights from Professor Glueck's book apply to both:

"Strategic Planning is that set of decisions and actions which leads to the development of an effective strategy or strategies to help achieve corporate objectives."

"- the firm chooses the most probable appraisal and diagnosis of the future environment (and future competitors) and of its own strengths and weaknesses. From this, it evolves the best strategy for this match of the environment and the firm."

"- analysis of the business and the preparation of several scenerios for the future. Contingency strategies are then prepared for each of these likely future scenerios."

"- A strategy is a unified, comprehensive, and integrated plan relating the strategic advantages of the firm to the challenges of the environment (competitors). It is designed to ensure that the basic objectives of the enterprise are achieved."

"The process of strategic planning is:

- Develop objectives

- Search the environment (including competitor competitive information and Benchmarking) and diagnose the significance of changes in

the economy, government/legal, market/competitive, supplier/techno-
logical, geographic and social factors.

- Examine and diagnose the significance of the size and distribution of
  the firm's resources, its strengths and weaknesses.

- Match the structure of the organization with the strategy."

"- a strategic quality plan has similarity with a "game plan" in sports.
Coaches examine a competitors past plans, strengths and weaknesses.
Then they look at their own teams strengths and weaknesses. The objective is to win the game. However a strategic quality plan is concerned
with future strengths and weaknesses and several competitors."

As a graduate of the Naval Academy in 1941, I was a member of
a rather large team that won the competition against Japan and Ger-
many for war. I am partial to a definition about strategic planning that
can be applied to competitions involving the economy. It is a quotation
from the greatest military leader the world has known, Chinese General Tsu, "Every battle is won before the battle is begun."

Through strategic quality planning, one can learn existing
strengths and weaknesses of one's own company, and anticipated
strengths and weaknesses of competitors, and make changes to acquire
greater strengths than competitors—before the competition begins.

Also, I have found it practical to give attention to another alleged
quotation from a prophet-turned-Admiral. Noah said, "I built the Ark
before it started to rain." It was Noah's way of saying, "Don't be too late
with too little."

Many officials initially underestimate the scope and magnitude of
the changes required, and the information essential to strategic quality
planning comes too late and is too little.

Relatively few company leaders choose approaches for strategic
quality planning that will insure achieving the company's needs and
expectations. Many other leaders are choosing approaches that will
not. Some best approaches follow.

***Building a Foundation Before Applying Malcolm Baldrige Guide-
lines:*** The rewards from building a foundation before applying the
Malcolm Baldrige guidelines have been addressed. A house can't be
constructed until the foundation is set in place. It is imperative to build
the foundation first.

The Consensus Approach: This approach is used by discussion
leaders at the Malcolm Baldrige Examiners Preparatory Course in the
evaluation and scoring of submissions, and in the preparation of feed-

back reports. A team of informed individuals, rather than one informed individual, will generate a large pool of information. They will generate more comprehensive findings and enhance the probability of providing the most important findings. Additional open discussions lead to a consensus on a few vital findings, or on scores.

Strategic quality planning requires the accumulation of considerable information, diagnosing the information, and determining the findings. The use of teams, instead of one individual, with the consensus approach can result in consensus on findings of greatest importance. This approach can also be used in self-evaluation and scoring to determine strengths and weaknesses for fulfilling the Malcolm Baldrige criteria, and provides a baseline for strategic quality planning.

Two-way Communication Between The Leader, Executives, Managers and Suppliers: Harvard Business Review Editor, and author of "The Changemasters," states, ". . . before improving quality or changing the culture or business direction, people at every level must understand and buy in on the vision."

The development of a strategic quality plan is dependent upon the involvement of many people. It's not only essential they buy in early, but the experience and ideas of executives, managers, and supplier officials must be mined to add perspective and contributions to the plan.

Encouragement by the top company leader for two-way open discussions with executives, managers and supplier officials can mine experience and ideas. Encouragement can build trust and avoid rumor that may lead to protectionism. It can achieve buy-in by those involved.

Establishing a Baseline: An evaluation and scoring of existing company strengths and areas needing improvement provide a baseline for strategic quality planning. The preparation of an early report such as that to apply for the National Quality Award, or conducting an extensive audit with a detailed written report, is time-consuming. A discussion leader, using detailed criteria, can query small teams of informed individuals and develop a consensus on strengths and weaknesses.

Evaluation And Scoring of Mythical Companies: The Examiner Preparatory Course uses cleverly prepared submissions from mythical companies as practice for evaluating and scoring against Malcolm Baldrige criteria. The practice includes development of a consensus on strengths and areas needing improvement and on scores for use in feedback reports.

Such reports from mythical companies along with a consensus reached for feedback reports can be procured from the Malcolm Baldrige Program Office or the American Society for Quality Control. A company can use this material to assist self-evaluation, learn desired strengths, and avoid weaknesses as part of the process for developing a strategic quality plan.

A Storehouse of Strengths: American business officials employed capitalism to create the greatest national economy the world has seen. Research this heritage. Recent American business leaders installed their individual versions of Total Quality and demonstrated success. Homework will reveal their strengths. Some of this knowledge is in the Appendix.

The Psychology About The Workplace For Developing a Strategic Quality Plan: I draw on my experience at General Electric, where we learned the importance of establishing a special location for the development of a strategic quality plan, and later, for monitoring progress in implementing the plan. We perfected what we appropriately called "The War Room." Four bare walls provided places to post missions, objectives, values, action plans, findings, and the essence of the plan. Several work tables provided places for teams to work, and for meetings with customers, suppliers, and union officials. The strategic business plan and the strategic quality plan were both developed in the same room, which greatly facilitated integration of the plans.

The self-esteem of the teams was enhanced. The neutral location avoided influence by individual organizations. Better two-way communication occurred at meetings between superiors and subordinates. The top official and executives feel liked, and become more involved. Supplier officials and union officials are impressed and comfortable at meetings and progress reviews. Customers, too, are very impressed and more likely to supply information about their needs and expectations.

Appendixes

The coauthors believe the body of this book describes the most advanced thinking about "What Total Quality Is" and "What Must Be Done To Establish It." Further, they have analyzed the visions and changes made by other officials who have established Total Quality at their companies and believe they have achieved general consensus about the visions and changes. But each company is different. Each has different products or services, different markets and customers, different competitors, and they come in different sizes and structures. They must adapt to meet their individual needs.

The coauthors have selected supplementary material from the best possible external sources to assist you adapt. They are categorized into the following Appendixes.

A. Foundations and Approaches of Selected Presidents and CEOs Who Have Installed Their Individual Versions of Total Quality.

B. Foundations and Approach in Japan by an Eminent Japanese Professor.

C. Perspective and Guidance From American's Internationally Recognized Quality Experts.

D. The Malcolm Baldrige National Quality Award by the Department of Common Associate Director.

Appendix A

Foundations and Approaches of Selected

Presidents and CEOs Who Have Installed Their

Individual Versions of Total Quality

JOHN YOUNG—HEWLETT PACKARD

The achievements of an organization are the result of the combined efforts of each individual in the organization working toward common objectives. These objectives should be realistic, should be clearly understood by everyone in the organization, and should reflect the organization's basic character and personality.

If the organization is to fulfill its objectives, it should strive to meet certain other fundamental requirements.

FIRST: The most capable people available should be selected for each assignment within the organization. Moreover, these people should have the opportunity—through continuing programs of training and education—to upgrade their skills and capabilities. This is especially important in a technical business where the rate of progress is rapid. Techniques that are good today will be outdated in the future, and people throughout the organization should continually be looking for new and better ways to do their work.

SECOND: Enthusiasm should exist at all levels. People in important management positions should not only be enthusiastic themselves, they should be selected for their ability to engender enthusiasm among their associates. There can be no place, especially among the people charged with management responsibility, for halfhearted interest or halfhearted effort.

THIRD: Even though an organization is made up of people fully meeting the first two requirements, all levels should work in unison toward common objectives and avoid working at cross purposes if the ultimate in efficiency and achievement is to be attained.

It has been our policy at Hewlett-Packard not to have a tight military type organization, but rather, to have overall objectives which are clearly stated and agreed to, and to give people the freedom to work toward those goals in ways they determine best for their own areas of responsibility.

OBJECTIVES:

1. PROFIT—To achieve sufficient profit to finance our company growth and to provide the resources we need to achieve our other corporate objectives.

2. CUSTOMERS—To provide products and services of the greatest possible value to our customers, thereby gaining and holding their respect and loyalty.

3. FIELDS OF INTEREST—To enter new fields only when the ideas we have, together with our technical manufacturing, and marketing skills, assure that we can make a needed and profitable contribution to the field.

4. GROWTH—To let our growth be limited only by our profits and our ability to develop and produce technical products that satisfy real customer needs.

5. OUR PEOPLE—To help HP people share in the company's success, which they make possible; to provide job security based on their performance; to recognize their individual achievements; and to insure the personal satisfaction that comes from a sense of accomplishment in their work.

6. MANAGEMENT—To foster initiative and creativity by allowing the individual great freedom of action in attaining well-defined objectives.

7. CITIZENSHIP—To honor our obligations to society by being an economic, intellectual, and social asset to each nation and each community in which we operate.

DAVID KEARNES—XEROX CORPORATION

The overall program is called "LEADERSHIP THROUGH QUALITY," a theme that came straight from the corporate boardroom through the policies set by David Kearns, chief executive officer. In early 1982, Kearns said, "We must create a Xerox team of employees whose energies and talents are challenged toward a common goal: that goal is quality in meeting the needs of internal and external customers. Quality is the basic business principle for Xerox and quality improvement is the job of every Xerox employee." The commitment to quality comes from the top, but it all started at the lower end of the corporation.

LEADERSHIP THROUGH QUALITY has three components: Employee Involvement, Competitive Benchmarking and the Quality Improvement Process. Each of the three strategies evolved for a different reason; each was a response to an overall need for quality programs.

Employee Involvement

Xerox faced two challenges in 1978 that demanded immediate attention. It had to recapture its lost market share and decrease the cost of doing business. Xerox was not selling its products cost effectively. In addition, there was a second, intangible problem even more significant than the short-term losses that were tracked on spread sheets: the intense competition and the company's loss of its leadership status affected employee morale.

A Quality Circles Program was begun to help solve both of these problems. Several employees visited Japan to observe Quality Circles in operation. While they were enthusiastic about the value of empowering employees, they hesitated at adopting the Japanese method wholesale. The six-step process that the team developed became the first major step in the EMPLOYEE INVOLVEMENT (EI) program in effect today.

Competitive Benchmarking

As the EI task force took the corporation through its first steps in problem solving, it became clear that a second process was needed to assure optimal results from the first. Thus a second task force was formed in late 1978 to create a competitive benchmarking strategy. Its goal was to assure the effectiveness of the first step of the problem-solving process. A performance standard was developed—that each function achieve and maintain superiority, or, at the very least, parity, in meeting customer requirements in every business activity.

Quality Improvement Process

The next step in the overall program was the implementation of a Business Effectiveness Plan. Initially the goals were defined as quality, productivity, and cost reduction. In late 1981, the Business Effectiveness strategy was redefined as consisting of three essentials: Quality Improvement, Employee Involvement and Competitive Benchmarking. This strategy was presented to 50 top executives, and less than a

year later, a complete LEADERSHIP THROUGH QUALITY STRAT-
EGY was conceived.

DONALD BEALL—ROCKWELL INTERNATIONAL

There are many excellent techniques for improving quality within any
organization. But the most basic requirement for quality—and perhaps the hardest to achieve—is an overall philosophy that encourages
the recognition of quality at every level, in every function, and by every
employee. Without that company-wide commitment, individual quality
improvement programs are likely to disappear with time. We have all
seen that happen.

Company-wide commitment is hard to achieve because it requires
ongoing involvement by management as well as enthusiastic participation by employees at all levels. In fact, one of the toughest parts about
adopting a philosophy of quality may be convincing employees that
you really mean it this time; they've got to know it's not just another
program that will run for six months or a year and then be dropped in
favor of a new buzz word. Quality efforts must result in a permanent
change in the way we design, manage, and produce—in the way we
meet our customers' needs.

All of us recognize that product quality is strategically important
to a company's long-term existence. Product quality has always been
important to the success of an enterprise, dating back to the time
craftsmen first stamped their hallmarks on product to indicate skilled
work. But in today's international, competitive environment quality is
absolutely vital—vital not only to the growth and profitability of the
enterprise but also to its long-term survival.

The days are long past when America's technological edge and its
industrial infrastructure overwhelm the rest of the world. Our international competitors have vigorously addressed quality and reliability
as strategic business issues for a long time. Quality isn't just another
program or a passing fad with them; it's a part of everything they do.
It dominates their thinking and every aspect of business from the
product design through manufacturing, through human resources,
service, and customer relationships. To be competitive, American
companies must make sure we're doing all of this and more. The
primary challenge for us as managers is to define our business quality
objectives and then meet them. We recognize that management
commitment from the top down is essential to creating a quality
culture and achieving quality objectives. But that commitment is only
a start.

Achieving quality excellence means moving beyond just making a formal commitment or issuing a policy or making a speech to the troops. Management has to take an active role in making things happen—getting involved and staying involved in the quality improvement process. I know a manager in one of our plants who got very much involved by actually going out and working a foreman's job for three or four weeks. It didn't take him long to see a lot of things that needed to be corrected. And since he's a bright guy, it didn't take him much longer to realize that a lot of the changes that needed to be made were things that he had vetoed as a plant manager.

Each of you has to make your own discoveries about the solutions that are right for your business. You don't have to switch jobs with the foreman to do it—but it might not hurt.

I've told our management team many times that there are no cookbook solutions to the challenges we face in our businesses. There is no magic recipe that will work for everybody in every instance. We have diverse businesses within Rockwell, both government and commercial, both domestic and international. Some of our businesses make a few highly complex products for one or two customers and others make thousands and thousands of identical products for hundreds of users.

We believe in trusting the managers of our business units and giving them the flexibility to direct their own efforts into committing resources as appropriate to focus attention on quality in their businesses. But at the same time, when it comes to the issue of quality improvement, it's important to accompany that freedom with direct day-to-day evidence of top management involvement. I've told the presidents of each Rockwell business unit that quality improvement must continue as a top-level priority for all functional units—for all employees within the company. It's a way of life.

Feedback is very important. Several senior executives and I conduct periodic productivity and quality reviews with the people who run each of our businesses. These sessions are usually four to five hours long. They explore in depth the issues facing each business and the actions that are being taken. They not only keep the managers on their toes, but also help sharpen the focus of all of our senior people in this critical area.

We've done a lot to leverage our technology and invest in capital improvements to enhance productivity and quality, as many of you have. We've added new plants, CAD/CAM, robotics, computers, office automation, and so on. We'll continue to make substantial investments of that type. But the robot hasn't been invented yet that can take the place of a really creative manager, or an enthusiastic and motivated individual. The attitudes and actions of our employees can provide quantum improvements in productivity and quality.

Too often when we talk about launching people programs, we make the mistake of aiming them only at the employees at the lowest level in the organization. Of course they must be included; they have to be a vital part of the team. But we need to focus more on active, ongoing participation by managers at all levels. Managers need to be in the position of encouraging every employe to be more innovative, more productive, more open, more candid, and more responsible—to feel accountable for making the business effective and successful. Managers need to lead by example; they need to communicate and motivate, not dictate. The employe should see by word and deed that the manager understands the job, understands the business, is open to suggestions and feedback, and has a deep personal commitment to quality in everything he or she does.

And I'm not just talking about the production area. I know that in many companies—certainly ours—most of the quality emphasis in the past has been in manufacturing. If we're doing things right, all company functions should have an equal responsibility for delivering products and services of excellent quality on time and on cost.

We've talked often about the lack of cooperation between labor and management over the years, and I think much of that is being rectified. An equally productive effort is being made to break down the functional barriers between engineering, manufacturing, quality, and marketing—to operate as a team, concentrating on beating competitors rather than each other. Such teamwork can leverage outstanding individual contributions and give a company the strength to meet and beat its competition. Teamwork becomes a force multiplier.

When you add it all up, what I'm saying is that management must create an environment in which quality in everything we do is a part of the culture and excellence is a virtue. Maybe that has been assumed in the past, but the goal today is to make it a recognized fact, not just an unspoken assumption. We need to have quality woven into the fabric of the way we manage every day, to have it fully supported, recognized, and rewarded by top management. This atmosphere for excellence has to start at the top of an organization and spread through each level. The quality attitude can be a shining light in the organization, but it's management's job to spark that flame.

DOUGLAS DANFORTH—WESTINGHOUSE ELECTRIC

It's often asked what the elements of our corporate strategy are. I define them this way: 1) Westinghouse is a diversified, technology-based corporation that competes on a worldwide basis. That's who we are; 2) We manage our resources in ways that continuously build value for our customers, our shareholders, and our employees. That's the result we seek; and 3) We manage our operations to achieve Total Quality in everything we do. That's how we get the results we seek. We portray Total Quality as a triangle.

The first element deals with results. The basic result of making Total Quality a corporate lifestyle is a competitive advantage worldwide.

The second element is measurement. These are the measurements we use to assess Total Quality performance. Two of them include the concept of value. The first, value-to-price ratio, is a measure of customer orientation. The second, value-to-cost ratio, is a measure of financial performance, which really addresses stockholder satisfaction. When these factors are expressed as targets, they become the requirement measurements of our organization.

The third element is the all important implementation phase— what our people have to do to make Total Quality happen. Our "how to do it" segment consists of four imperatives. They are: customer orientation, human resource excellence, product/process leadership, and management leadership.

We characterize these imperatives by what we call the twelve conditions of excellence—conditions that must be met to fulfill Total Quality requirements. We've classified the conditions by how they support our four implementation imperatives.

The first layer is customer orientation.

The customer is where it all starts. The key focus is on value. That means knowing what our customer needs and wants are, and successfully translating that knowledge into the operating requirements of our business.

The second imperative, human resource excellence, is more than just people. It also deals with their participation, their continuing education and training, and their motivation.

The third implementation building block is product/process leadership. This imperative dictates that we pay close attention to products and services, as well as processes and procedures, information and suppliers.

The fourth and final element of Total Quality, management leadership, is the foundation on which everything rests. It requires a vision, a new orientation—a new way for everyone to do his or her job.

ROBERT TALLON—FLORIDA POWER & LIGHT

. . . the best way I know to hold on to a customer is with quality. . .

Let me begin by declaring that the quality improvement imperative is not a fad. A lot of us thought it was, when it was first introduced into our company. As one of the speakers said this morning, we thought that if we kept quiet, it would go away. But it hasn't. In fact, I believe it's the most valuable management system ever employed by our company. The return on your investment in quality improvement begins the very instant that your company makes a commitment to do things right—not just better, but right. Thomas Edison pinpointed exactly what I'm talking about when he said that discontent is the first necessity of progress. Edison went a step further and, as usual, he didn't pull any punches; he said, "There is a better way. Find it." I guess we've all been trying to find a better way for a long time, Florida Power and Light Company included. At FPL, we were searching to find a better way, even while much of America was convinced that care and craftsmanship went out of style with the Frigidaire and came back in with the Toyota.

For a while, we presumed what many others have presumed, that quality is free. But we discovered that quality is about as free as clean air and about as difficult to grasp. In 1981 we began revival of quality at FPL, with a company-wide movement centered on the quality improvement program which we simply called QIP. QIP is not free either. And QIP calls for nothing less than total commitment on the part of management. We have about 2.7 million customers at FPL and we sell them a heck of a lot of electricity, but we don't have to sell quality to a single customer. The great thing about quality is that all you have to do is produce it and then it's going to take care of itself.

But what is the return on investment of producing quality—and when do you start seeing the results? Who benefits, and how is it measured? The initial investment that I alluded to—the idea of doing it right—is something more valuable than money. That is a difficult concept for some of us to accept and perhaps even more difficult for some of our shareholders to understand. But how do we attach a price to a complete change of attitude? A changing corporate culture that espouses not only a philosophy with a new respect for quality, but a new respect for the customer as well? How much is it worth to you, and to the stockholders, to be able to create within your company an environment where positive change is encouraged and quality performance is expected, where waste and inefficiency are viewed as undesirable and unacceptable by virtually every employee? Such an environment, in my mind at least, is priceless. It's the commitment to quality that I believe is essential not only for the bottom line, but for our very survival as a business, and perhaps as a nation.

This sweeping statement is especially true in a service industry like mine, where the bottom-line impact is often difficult to evaluate. Yet that bottom-line impact does exist, and we cannot afford to ignore it.

It's a bottom line that in our business exists as much for our customers as for our stockholders. We're a rapidly changing industry. We're no longer a monopoly in the classical sense. Competition is charging towards us. And the best way I know to hold on to a customer is with quality—a quality product, quality service, and quality management. Our company-wide quality improvement program is only five years old, but I'm proud to point out that already it has become an internationally recognized, award-winning program. We have had more than 400 American companies and organizations visit our company to seek guidance in their own efforts towards quality improvement.

While that's tremendously gratifying to us, I must admit it's not a surprise. Our very first limited quality improvement efforts went into the building of our nuclear power plants in the mid-1970s, and the results were dramatic. We achieved a breakthrough for excellence that allowed us to build, test, and license a nuclear unit in a record time of six years, when the national average was around ten years. It was an accomplishment that saved our company and our customers over $600 million in building, labor, and financing costs.

But we knew we had a tiger by the tail in QIP; the trick was to get the tiger into the tank. We needed more than just a tune-up or an oil change, we needed a major overhaul. We had to change not only the way we did things, but the way we thought about doing things. And initially we looked at the very simple things, the problems on which our people could develop their skills in QIP.

Today, we're seeking breakthroughs, innovative ways of doing business that can help keep the increase in rates at or below the consumer price index, as well as provide an increased return on investment to our stockholders. And by the first part of 1989, we expect to be looking for breakthroughs that will help us solve major problems and expand to new opportunities. You know, "breakthrough" is kind of a corporate buzzword today. I don't believe it's anything much more than a new idea—or sometimes even an old idea with new applications. And it doesn't take very many such ideas to achieve success. As Albert Einstein admitted, he had only one great idea in his entire lifetime, but his theory of relativity kept him in pipe tobacco for a heck of a lot of years.

While we may be some distance away from achieving the major breakthroughs that are the ultimate stepping stones of quality, the program is more than paying its own way, even at these early stages. While our costs will continue to come down as our training takes effect, our savings will continue to go up as our people become more efficient and more knowledgeable about quality. Furthermore, we expect major breakthroughs in the future to add to our savings.

In the minds of most folks, quality at FPL is synonymous with the reliability of our product. If the power comes on and stays on at the flick of a switch, that's quality to most of our customers. But quality runs much deeper than that, and one of the greatest risks that we face in evaluating any quality program is to overlook the long-range results. As an example, we put off building new power plants, hoping to delay as long as possible the tremendous costs involved: despite steady growth in number of customers as well as customer demand, we don't anticipate building new power plants until perhaps 1994 or thereabouts; and we are one of the fastest growing utilities in the nation. That presents an obvious challenge to keep our old power plants running efficiently, and quality maintenance is what's going to make that happen—and what's going to make our customers happy with us.

Our quality improvement program is made up of three continuing phases, each totally independent of the other. The first was the quality circle. We have 1,700 teams and some 8,000 employees taking part in that process, but we believe that the quality circle only scratches the surface of potential for quality improvement. We're already implementing the second phase—the corporate goal-setting phase—which we call policy deployment. The third phase, which we're now beginning, is called quality in daily work—a way of applying the QIP concepts to everyday normal work. Our schedule is to have all three phases in action some time in 1989.

It's our intention to infuse the process and the philosophy of QIP into every corporate cubbyhole at FPL, to weave the process and philosophy so deeply into the fiber of doing business that it becomes second nature to each and every employee. Lately, the idea of American quality has become somewhat of a myth, and the trouble with myths is that someone might begin to believe them. And I don't think we can accept that myth as a company—and I know that we cannot accept it as a nation—if we wish to maintain and indeed build upon our role as a world economic force.

Our service representatives have taken to heart the idea of staying with the problem—and the customer—until the problem is solved and the customer is satisfied. Those are the kinds of results that we're looking for in QIP—the kinds of return on investment that may not show up on the ledger but are vital to our company's future well-being. A part of our quality improvement program features a corporate vision which is simply this: during the next decade, we want to become the best-managed utility in the U.S. and to be recognized as such. Just this summer, we were fortunate enough to be named winner of the Edison Award—the highest honor given within our industry—and QIP was highlighted as the single most significant contribution to serving our customers effectively.

The Edison Award brings to mind the fact that Edison, like a number of you, was a customer of FPL for many years. I'm not sure, if Edison were alive, that I'd have the nerve to send him a bill. Instead, I might send him a note thanking him for the bit of advice he gave so many years ago—I suppose it wasn't so much a piece of advice as a directive: "There is a better way. Find it."

At FPL we're a long way from reaching the end of our journey toward total quality, but I believe we are beginning to see the light at the end of the tunnel. And though I can't predict when quality improvement will give you the return on investment you may be looking for, I sincerely believe that the quality concept can mold the corporate future of America.

RICHARD THOMAS—FIRST CHICAGO

The success of our quality program within our service products group alone is telling proof that providing excellent products and services and containing costs can be mutually compatible efforts.

During the past decade or so, new technologies, new products, and new competitors have brought enormous change to financial services. Yet there are some things that haven't changed in banking—the most important being bankers' fiduciary responsibilities to their customers. Another element that has remained constant over the years is the fact that banking is a business built on credibility, trust, and good faith; when there is a breach in any one of these areas, the effects on a financial institution are invariably damaging and of long duration. In light of the strong and growing competition in financial services, it is also true that today bankers must always seek to provide customers with an extra measure of value. We must remind ourselves again and again that the customer is paramount and we must act accordingly.

At First Chicago, we are especially conscious of the importance of quality. We give it extremely close attention because it flows from our number one bank-wide commitment, which is that the customer is our highest priority. Every person who joins our bank is made aware of that right away, and is reminded of it regularly. We firmly believe that our commitment to our customers must be shared by every one of our employees. We also know that we simply can't compete in today's financial services marketplace if we don't provide consistently superior products and services. Today's business environment is much less forgiving, and customers are much too knowledgeable, sophisticated, and yes, demanding as well, for any enterprise—especially a bank—to take quality for granted.

In *A Passion for Excellence,* Tom Peters and Nancy Austin assert that there are really only two ways to achieve and sustain outstanding performance over the long term: you have to take exceptional care of your customers through superior service and superior quality and you have to innovate constantly. This past spring, we at First Chicago carried out a major repositioning of our corporate banking business; that restructuring was consistent with the common sense behind those two rules of thumb. Each of you knows that your own company's financial needs are becoming more complex with each passing day. Even before we refined our organizational structure, we talked to many of our customers; like you, they wanted high-quality advice, high-quality products and services, and flawlessly executed transactions. Our reorganization became a vehicle for strengthening First Chicago's ability to meet those very needs.

In order to serve our large corporate customers most effectively, we established a new entity that brings together all the groups in our organization that serve the large corporate marketplace. We call it the "global corporate bank," and it is being managed as a partnership within a corporate structure.

The basic unit within our corporate bank is the client service team. This team is led by a relationship manager who works shoulder to shoulder with all the necessary product specialists. Each client service team includes a senior individual who frequently is a partner in our global corporate bank. In fact, all nine of our partners serve as managers of relationships to underscore our commitment to the customer.

The significance to our customers of this approach to banking is that they have more and faster access to very senior officers, who have the knowledge, experience, and authority to provide top-flight financial assistance promptly. Our new arrangement also provides a convenient mechanism for individuals on a client service team to share their knowledge of the customer, and by doing that, to anticipate better the customer's future requirements for financial products and services, as well as better serve their current needs.

In addition to providing our global corporate customers with commercial and investment banking services, we also offer them a range of traditional operating products, which are often termed cash management services. It has become essential that clients move and manage money and information swiftly. Among the operating products we provide are payment systems, remittance processing services, information products, and shareholder services. The business unit that generates these products and services—a unit within our global corporate bank—is the service products group. This group demonstrates in quantifiable terms the power and reach of a thoughtfully planned and vigorously applied quality program.

By way of background, I might note that the operating products departments within banks traditionally were cost centers. Cash management services were loss leaders, if you will; banks essentially gave these services away in the hopes of making a profit on the credit products provided as part of the overall customer relationship.

In light of the dual trend toward thinner margins on the credit side of our business and toward the unbundling of financial products and services, we saw both a need and an opportunity to turn that cost center into a profit center, by taking full advantage of the fee-generating potential of top-flight operating products.

Five years ago, we set out to be the quality provider of cash management services. Yet we knew at the time that we couldn't achieve that goal without a serious quality assurance program. Our very first step was to bring on board, to head our service products group, someone who not only had a comprehensive knowledge of operating products but also a rock-solid commitment to quality. The next step in developing our quality program was to change our organizational framework within the service products group and within other areas of the bank. We did this by creating separate strategic business units—SBUs—each of which concentrated on an individual product family. We vested each SBU manager with the power to control not only the expenses for each operating product, but also pricing, product features, promotion, and quality, thus giving each manager the necessary tools to meet the customer's requirements.

Our next task was to identify in concrete terms those customer requirements: by asking and listening, we learned that prominent among our clients' needs and expectations are timeliness, accuracy, efficiency, responsive service, and good communication. Given this information, we wanted to make sure that we were indeed satisfying these customer requirements. We also wanted to dispel the belief held by many people that quality is difficult to measure in a service environment. So we subsequently developed an extensive performance measurement system that tracks on a weekly basis some 700 indicators that customers consider important.

Drawing from customer expectations and from industry standards, we established levels of minimum acceptable performance for each of our operating products; in addition, we set goals for exceptional performance. At weekly performance meetings, data on how we are doing relative to these demanding goals are charted and presented to senior management. What is more, the goals are revised upward on a regular basis. We do all of this measuring and charting not simply to encourage in-house competition, nor do we do this solely to provide management information; rather, the chief reason we measure and chart and analyze is to bring about improvement. The information we're generating from this process gives us an early warning that something is amiss and allows us to take corrective actions faster.

These weekly meetings that measure quality are extremely useful for another reason. We regularly invite our customers, and even our suppliers, to attend them. There is a two-fold benefit in doing this. First, we have an additional forum in which to learn about customers' expectations and concerns involving our products and services, and we use that knowledge to refine and improve both. The second benefit is that we are sending a loud and clear and sincere message that the customer is our central interest.

This quality program, of which these weekly meetings are just one element, has had a tremendous impact on our performance. For example, back in 1982, our remittance banking lock-box operation experienced one error in every 4,000 transactions. Today that figure is one in 10,000. Just two years ago, our average processing time for a telephone money transfer was 20 minutes. Presently, only 13 minutes elapse between the time we receive a telephone order and the time of final execution of the transfer.

Customer feedback about the quality initiatives within our service products area has been extremely positive. We couldn't be happier about that, yet we have no intention of resting on our successes. Recent findings published by a major independent research firm help explain why. Their data show that the key controlled buying determinants for noncredit services are quality and service. And when the researchers asked customers of banks to cite the problems that jeopardize banking relationships, two items were mentioned most often: operating errors and slow problem correction. Both of these are quality issues, pure and simple.

The success of our quality program within our service products group alone is telling proof that providing excellent products and services and containing costs can be mutually compatible efforts. In fact, we've learned firsthand that an emphasis on quality is one of the most effective ways to control costs. For example, generally speaking, it costs us something less than $10 to execute a money transfer—that is, if we do it right the first time. If we don't, if the money is sent to the wrong place or doesn't get there on time or if there's some other problem, the average cost of correcting an error is over $400. The exact figure depends on the amount of money involved and complexities of the situation and so forth, but as an average figure, that's pretty dramatic.

Overall, the quality program of our service products group results in documented savings of $7–10 million annually—and I suspect the true figure is really much higher than that. The cost reductions that this group has realized have also allowed prices for our cash management services to remain relatively constant over the past few years, giving us a better competitive position in the marketplace.

These cost savings are important for another reason. More and more corporate treasurers are looking at the total cost of using one cash management service over another. The bank with the lowest per-item price might actually be much more expensive to use if its error rate is high. So by reducing our error rate, we also have lowered the overall cost to our customers when they do business with us.

Of course, high quality, customer satisfaction, and competitive prices also translate into repeat business, referrals, and new business, making the quality investment an even wiser one. We at First Chicago are convinced that a strategy based on quality is the best way that any company in any business can respond to competition. Yet it is also terribly important from a marketing perspective to communicate that quality commitment to the marketplace. Our relationship managers receive regular information on our quality program and its effectiveness, and help carry that information to the corporate community. Each year we also send to our customers a comprehensive booklet of key performance measurement charts, so that they can see the indicators we monitor and how our bank performs in these areas. The quality theme also is woven into all of our product brochures. To be truly effective, the quality imperative has to be integrated into the entire organization, because success will be incomplete and short-lived if the commitment to quality is anything but company-wide.

By focusing on our service products group, I don't want to leave you with the notion that quality initiatives are any less prominent or less supported in our other business areas. For example, quality assurance is an integral part of our commercial lending activities. Two years ago, we instituted a credit process review system that takes a smarter and more comprehensive look at asset quality, in terms of who we lend to and how we manage loans once they are made. We try to identify our risks at the very start and we hold each division responsible for the loans it generates, thus increasing accountability. The result is that it is now much easier to spot problems when they first appear and to apply corrective measures immediately.

Our credit process review system is highly analytical, but at the same time, highly sensitive to the particulars of the customer's situation. Our commercial lending philosophy is based on establishing and nurturing what we expect will be long-term relationships. On the other hand, when such a long-term relationship cannot be developed or sustained, then we seek to disengage in a professional way. A quality lending operation has many facets—and is difficult to measure or define in any precise way—but it is very important, because the cost of poor loan decisions is very high.

In our middle-market business, which is represented primarily by our subsidiary, American National Corporation, the quality imperative must also run strong. I say "must" because serving this sector of the corporate marketplace well is not an easy undertaking. I'm talking about companies with sales in the $5 million to $120 million range. Serving this market requires an intimate knowledge of the businesses and owners who make up this market, because middle market customers seek a special degree of trust and service from their bankers. These customers—who rely heavily on banks for credit and other financial services—seek close contact and long-standing commitments, so when quality falters on the banker's part, the effect is especially evident in this environment.

We are also committed to delivering quality services in our third major business, consumer banking. That area also has a host of quality procedures and programs in place:

- Quality teams that address specific customer issues and problems.

- An action center that handles extraordinary problems.

- A quality task force led by the department head.

- Customer roundtable luncheons, held at our bank, as well as employee roundtables.

- Newsletters, brochures, and other literature devoted to quality issues.

In addition, our credit card, another part of our consumer banking business, owes much of its successful performance to quality control programs.

Our objective throughout the bank is to make every employee accountable for quality. We want to raise each employee's quality consciousness, if you will, so that the provision of top-flight customer service is a reflex action. We believe that the quality mandate has to come from the top—that's essentially a given. Yet it's equally important that top management defines what it means by quality. We all know that people work better and smarter with specific, well-defined goals and guidelines, whether those goals involve quality or anything else.

And when senior managers send a clear signal that top quality performance is not just hoped for, but absolutely expected, people generally respond by aspiring to that expectation. Employees very naturally begin to attach more importance to their work when others, namely senior managers, view employee work as important. Stated another way, nothing does more to destroy good performance in the workplace than the perception, real or imagined, that management is indifferent to quality.

The pursuit of quality generates its own momentum, we've found, so that quality begets quality. Smart companies know this, and they also know that every dollar spent on good quality assurance programs will yield abundant returns. Quite literally, it really pays to do it right the first time.

APPENDIX B

Perspective and Guidance from America's

Internationally Recognized Quality Experts

Quality, the cornerstone of competitive strategy for firms that hope to survive the 20th century, is having a profound effect on the way companies are managed. American business is being drawn into the quality revolution by the ever-growing expectations of customers around the world, who are demanding high-quality products and services at low prices. For those that succeed, the evidence shows clearly that quality has become the key to increasing both market share and profits.

While some U.S. firms have turned to promotional gimmicks to improve their quality image, many are making dramatic changes and finding that a real commitment to meeting higher quality goals also results in higher productivity, thereby lowering costs.

A small group of "quality experts" have been saying for years that quality is a cost effective and necessary business strategy. Today, a growing number of U.S. firms are following the coaching of these experts in an effort to compete. Four of the most sought after "quality coaches" are W. Edwards Deming, Joseph M. Juran, William E. Conway, and Philip B. Crosby.

All of them recognize that there are no short cuts to quality, and that the improvement process is a never-ending cycle, requiring the full support and participation of individual workers, whole departments, and, most importantly, top management. Beyond that, the four coaches disagree about how best to go about improving quality. This report presents their individual "game plans" for American business.

Dr. W. Edwards Deming

Dr. W. Edwards Deming is the 85-year-old statistician best known for setting Japanese business upon the course that has made them number one in quality throughout the world. In 1950, he went to Japan to help the U.S. Secretary of War conduct a population census, and was invited to lecture to top business leaders on statistical quality control. Deming told the Japanese they could "take over the world" if they followed his advice. The rest is history, and today the highest quality award in Japan is named after Deming. He has been called the "founder of the Third Wave of the Industrial Revolution," and often sounds like a crusader for quality with statements such as, "it is time to adopt a new religion in America."

He estimates that it will take the United States 30 years to accomplish what the Japanese have done to improve quality because "a big ship, travelling at full speed, requires distance and time to turn." He warns that "people who expect quick results are doomed to disappointment."

According to Deming, good quality does not necessarily mean high quality. It is, rather, "a predictable degree of uniformity and dependability, at low cost, and suited to the market." He recognizes that the quality of any product or service has many scales, and may get a high mark on one scale and a low mark on another. In other words, quality is whatever the customer needs and wants. And since the customer's requirements and tastes are always changing, the solution to defining quality in terms of the customer is to constantly conduct customer research.

Deming's basic philosophy on quality is that productivity improves as variability decreases. Since all things vary, he says, that is why the statistical method of quality control is needed. "Statistical control does not imply absence of defective items. It is a state of random variation, in which the limits of variation are predictable," he explains.

There are two types of variation: chance and assignable, and says Deming, "The difference between these is one of the most difficult things to comprehend." It is a waste of time and money to look for the cause of chance variation, yet, he says, this is exactly what many companies do when they attempt to solve quality problems without using statistical methods. He advocates the use of statistics to measure performance in all areas, not just conformance to product specifications. Furthermore, he says it is not enough to meet specifications; one has to keep working to reduce the variation as well.

Deming is extremely critical of U.S. management and is an advocate of worker participation in decision making. He claims that management is responsible for 94 percent of quality problems, and points out that it is management's task to help people work smarter, not harder. "The first step is for management to remove the barriers that rob the hourly worker of his right to do a good job," he says.

He also knocks motivational programs, in which he includes zero defects, and says that everyone simply doing their best is not the answer because it is also necessary that people know what to do. And, he asks, "How can a man do it right the first time when the incoming material is off gauge, off color, or otherwise defective, or if his machine is not in good order?"

Deming cites the following as a typical letter from a supplier in response to an inquiry on its quality: "We are pleased to inform you that quality is our motto. We believe in quality. You will see from the enclosed pamphlet that nothing goes out of this plant until it has been thoroughly inspected. In fact, a large portion of our effort in production is spent on inspection to be sure of our quality." This, he says, "is a true confession of ignorance of what quality is, and how to achieve it."

Inspection, whether of incoming or outgoing goods, is, according to Deming, too late, ineffective, and costly. "Inspection does not improve quality, nor guarantee it," he says. Moreover, inspection is usually designed to allow a certain number of defects to enter the system. For example, a company that buys items with an acceptable quality level of three percent is, in effect, telling the vendor that it can send three bad items out of every 100. "The vendor will be pleased to meet these requirements," says Deming.

He says that judging quality requires knowledge of the "statistical evidence of quality," and that companies dealing with vendors under statistical control can eliminate inspection. "You will note from the control charts that came along with the product, far better than any inspection can tell you, what the distribution of quality is, and what it will be tomorrow." In this way, quality is predictable, and one can also safely predict that the vendor's quality will improve over time. "One of the first steps for managers of purchasing to take is to learn enough about the statistical control of quality to be able to assess the qualifications of a supplier, to be able to talk to him in statistical language," says Deming.

Deming also points out that simply checking the specifications of incoming materials may not be enough if the material encounters problems in production. "Specifications cannot tell the whole story. The supplier must know what the material is to be used for," he says.

He is critical of most procedures for qualifying vendors on quality because once qualified, the vendor "has discharged his responsibility, and the purchaser accepts whatever he gets." The only effective way to qualify vendors is to see if their management abides by his 14 points, uses statistical process control, and is willing to cooperate on tests and use of instruments and gauges.

The best recognition one can give a quality vendor, according to Deming, is to give that vendor more business. He points out that requiring statistical evidence of process control in selecting vendors would mean, in most companies, a drastic reduction in the number of vendors they deal with simply because not that many vendors would qualify. Nevertheless, he says, this is the only way to choose vendors, even if that means relying on a single source for critical items. In fact,

Deming advocates single sourcing. "A second source, for protection, for every item purchased is a costly practice," he says. The advantages of single sourcing include better vendor commitment, eliminating small differences between products from two suppliers, and simplifying accounting and paperwork.

As to the fact that relying on a single source can often mean paying a higher price, Deming says, "The policy of forever trying to drive down the price of anything purchased, with no regard to quality and service, can drive good vendors and good service out of business. The ways of doing business with vendors and customers that were good enough in the past must now be revised to meet new requirements of quality and productivity."

Deming works as a private consultant to dozens of firms in the United States. It is said that he will simply stop working with a client who does not show a total commitment to quality.

Deming's 14 Points for Management

1. Create constancy of purpose toward improvement of product and service.

2. Adopt the new philosophy. We can no longer live with commonly accepted levels of delays, mistakes, defective materials, and defective workmanship.

3. Cease dependence on mass inspection. Require instead statistical evidence that quality is built in.

4. End the practice of awarding business on the basis of price tag.

5. Find problems. It is management's job to work continually on the system.

6. Institute modern methods of training on the job.

7. Institute modern methods of supervision of production workers. The responsibility of foremen must be changed from numbers to quality.

8. Drive out fear, so that everyone may work effectively for the company.

9. Break down barriers between departments.

10. Eliminate numerical goals, posters and slogans for the work force, asking for new levels of productivity without providing methods.

11. Eliminate work standards that prescribe numerical quotas.

12. Remove banners that stand between the hourly worker and his right to pride of workmanship.

13. Institute a vigorous program of education and training.

14. Create a structure in top management that will push every day on the above 13 points.

Joseph M. Juran

Joseph M. Juran was born 81 years ago in Rumania, and came to the United States in 1912. After studying electrical engineering and law, he rose to chief of the inspection control division of Western Electric Co. and professor at New York University. Juran, like Deming, is credited with part of the quality success story of Japan, where he went in 1954 to lecture on how to manage for quality. He is the author of numerous books on quality and management, as well as editor of the /w/Quality Control Handbook.' In 1979, he founded the Juran Institute, which conducts quality training seminars.

According to Juran, there are two kinds of quality: "fitness for use" and "conformance to specifications." To illustrate the difference, he says a dangerous product could meet all specifications, but not be fit for use.

Juran was the first to deal with the broad management aspects of quality, which distinguishes him from those who espouse specific techniques, statistical or otherwise. In the 1940's, he pointed out that the technical aspects of quality control had been well covered, but that firms did not know how to manage for quality. He identified some of the problems as organization, communication, and coordination of functions—in other words, the human element. According to Juran, "An understanding of the human situations associated with the job will go far to solve the technical problems; in fact such understanding may be a prerequisite of a solution." For example, an inspector may incorrectly interpret the specifications and thus subvert quality control efforts, or worse, he may knowingly protect favored operators or suppliers.

Juran talks about three basic steps to progress: structured annual improvements combined with devotion and a sense of urgency, massive training programs, and upper management leadership. In his view less than 20% of quality problems are due to workers, with the remainder being caused by management. Just as all managers need some training in finance, all should have training in quality in order to oversee and participate in quality improvement projects. And *top* management should be included because, "all major quality problems are interdepartmental." Moreover, pursuing departmental goals can sometimes undermine a company's overall quality mission, he says.

Companies should avoid "campaigns to motivate the workforce to solve the company's quality problems by doing perfect work," says Juran, because these "exhortation only" approaches and slogans "fail to set specific goals, establish specific plans to meet these goals, or provide the needed resources." He notes, however, that upper managers like these programs because they do not detract from their time.

Juran favors the concept of quality circles because they improve communications between management and labor. He also recommends using statistical process control, but warns that it can lead to a "tool-oriented" approach. Juran does not believe that "quality is free." He explains that because of the law of diminishing returns, there is an optimum point of quality, beyond which conformance is more costly than the value of the quality obtained.

He recognizes purchasing's important role in quality improvement. "A company cannot produce greater precision in *vacuo;* it must secure greater precision from its suppliers." Juran also recognizes that purchasing's task can be much more complex than ordinarily assumed. For example, he addresses the problems of assessing the quality of contractors competing for big one-of-a-kind projects, as well as how to deal with unexpected changes in specifications.

Typical of his penchant for looking at the "big picture," Juran points out that at the same time that buyers are recognizing the need for better communications with suppliers, more and more of these suppliers are foreign firms. This puts up potential barriers to communications due to language and other cultural differences. He also points to different technological standards throughout the world and the fact that international standardization is lengthy and slow.

Juran is not in favor of single sourcing for important purchases, which he defines as product-related items such as raw materials or components. "For important purchases it is well to use multiple sources of supply. A single source can more easily neglect to sharpen its competitive edge in quality, cost, and service," he says.

Training for purchasing managers should include techniques for rating vendors, according to Juran, and he adds that rating vendors is only half of the process. The customer must also "make the investment of time, effort, and special skills to help the poor vendors improve."

To qualify vendors on quality, purchasing needs to do a formal survey to insure that the vendor can consistently manufacture to specifications. Comparing U.S. and Japanese vendor qualifying practices, Juran says those in the United States are not as effective. "To predict vendor adequacy, U.S. firms studied the suppliers' systems—organization, written procedures, manuals, audits, and so on. The Japanese firms looked at process capabilities, process controls, acceptance of teamwork relationships, extent of quality control training, and quality of prior deliveries." He is critical of arms-length and adversary relationships with vendors, and says they should be part of the team.

The Juran Institute teaches a project-by-project, problem-solving, team method of quality improvement, in which upper management must be involved. "The project approach is important. When it comes to quality, there is no such thing as improvement in general. Any improvement in quality is going to come about project by project and no other way," says Juran.

Juran's 10 Steps to Quality Improvement

1. Build awareness of the need and opportunity for improvement.

2. Set goals for improvement.

3. Organize to reach the goals (establish a quality council, identify problems, select projects, appoint teams, designate facilitators).

4. Provide training.

5. Carry out projects and solve problems.

6. Report progress.

7. Give recognition.

8. Communicate results.

9. Keep score.

10. Maintain momentum by making annual improvement part of the regular systems and processes of the company.

Philip B. Crosby

Philip B. Crosby is the 59-year-old quality expert best known for coming up with the concept of zero defects in the early 1960's when he was in charge of quality for the Pershing missile project at Martin Corp. In 1965, he went to ITT as director of quality, and left in 1979 to form Philip Crosby Associates. He got into consulting and writing because "I was tired of hearing how the United States was going down the chute." His book, 'Quality Is Free,' has sold more than one million copies.

According to Crosby's definition, quality is conformance to requirements, and it can only be measured by the cost of nonconformance. "Don't talk about poor quality or high quality. Talk about conformance and nonconformance," he says. This approach means that the only standard of performance is zero defects.

If he had to sum up in a single word what quality management is all about, Crosby says the word would be "prevention." Whereas the conventional view says quality is achieved through inspection, testing, and checking, he says that prevention is the only system that can be utilized. And when Crosby says "prevention" he means "perfection." There is no place in his philosophy for statistically acceptable levels of quality. "People go to great elaborate things to develop statistical levels of compliance. We've learned to believe that error is inevitable, and to plan for it." But, he says, "There is absolutely no reason for having errors or defects in any product."

Crosby talks about a quality "vaccine" that firms can use to prevent nonconformances. The three ingredients of this vaccine are determination, education, and implementation. He points out that quality improvement is a process not a program, saying, "Nothing permanent or lasting ever comes from a program."

He says quality is management's responsibility, and that "We have to be as concerned about quality as we are about profit." He is doubtful, however, that this change in attitude will occur in this generation because most companies continue to compound quality problems by "hassling" their employees, which renders them demotivated by the "thoughtless, irritating, unconcerned way they are dealt with." Crosby says a committed management can obtain a 40 percent reduction in error rates very quickly from a committed workforce, while eliminating the remaining error takes a little more work.

One misconception concerning Crosby is that he is primarily advocating prodding workers into performing better. He explains the root of this misconception, saying, "Unfortunately, zero defects was pick up by industry as a 'motivation' program." In 1964, the Japanese adopted zero defects, and Crosby says they were the only ones who correctly applied it—as a management performance standard rather than a motivation program for employees.

Crosby says that in purchased items, at least half of quality problems are caused by not clearly stating what the requirements are. Since defects are defined as deviations from the published, announced, or agreed-upon requirements, a lot of effort and thought should go into those requirements. In this, he points to the example of Japan, where "they treat the supplier as an extension of their own business."

As it is now, he says, "Half of the rejections that occur are the fault of the purchaser." For this reason, Crosby recommends rating buyers as well as vendors. "In tracking purchasing agents you find that they have a built in defect rate," he explains.

Visiting a potential supplier to conduct a quality audit is next to useless, according to Crosby. "Unless the vendor is a complete and obvious disaster area, it is impossible to know whether their quality system will provide the proper control or not."

Philip Crosby Associates offers company-wide training through its Quality College, and is now expanding from management training to supplying training materials and training instructors.

Crosby's 14 Steps to Quality Improvement

1. Make it clear that management is committed to quality.
2. Form quality improvement teams with representatives from each department.
3. Determine where current and potential quality problems lie.
4. Evaluate the cost of quality and explain its use as a management tool.
5. Raise the quality awareness and personal concern of all employees.
6. Take actions to correct problems identified through previous steps.
7. Establish a committee for the zero defects program.
8. Train supervisors to actively carry out their part of the quality improvement programs.
9. Hold a zero defects day to let all employees realize that there has been a change.
10. Encourage individuals to establish improvement goals for themselves and their groups.
11. Encourage employees to communicate to management the obstacles they face in attaining their improvement goals.
12. Recognize and appreciate those who participate.
13. Establish quality councils to communicate on a regular basis.
14. Do it all over again to emphasize that the quality improvement program never ends.

William E. Conway

William E. Conway is a relative newcomer to the quality game. Born 60 years ago, he graduated from Harvard and the U.S. Naval Academy before beginning a business career that would lead him to the top as president and chairman of Nashua Corp. In 1979, he invited Dr. Deming to Nashua Corp. to help improve the firm's quality. The visits lasted three years, and in 1983, he founded Conway Quality, Inc. Because of his close association with Deming, he is sometimes described as a "Deming disciple," but Conway has developed his own plan for quality improvement.

He does not talk in terms of a specific definition of quality per se. Instead, he incorporates that into his broad definition of quality management, which he says is "development, manufacture, administration, and distribution of consistent low cost products and services that customers want and/or need." Quality management also means constant improvement in all areas of operations, including suppliers and distributors, to eliminate waste of material, capital, and time. The wasting of time is, by far, the biggest waste that occurs in most organizations, according to Conway. Excess inventory is another important form of waste because, he says, 60 percent of the space commonly used is not needed, yet a company must pay for it, pay to maintain it, and pay taxes on it.

Taking the view of the man who has been there at the top of a corporation, Conway talks about the "right way to manage" rather than simply how to improve quality. He says the biggest problem is that top management is not convinced that quality increases productivity and lowers costs. Furthermore, they feel they don't have time to deal with the problem. "The bottleneck is located at the top of the bottle."

What is required is the creation of a new "system of management," whose primary task is continuous improvement in all areas. This, he says, is the most important change, and means changing all the unwritten rules in a company, and giving people positive reinforcement. "People work *in* the system, management works *on* the system. Workers will welcome the change," promises Conway. And while critical of U.S. management, he recognizes that "management wants and needs real help—not destructive criticism."

Conway is a strong advocate of using statistical methods to achieve quality gains, and says that one of the greatest handicaps lies in attempting to deal with productivity and quality in generalities. "The use of statistics is a common sense way of getting into specifics," he says, adding, "Statistics don't solve problems. They identify where the problems are and point managers and workers towards solutions."

He distinguishes between simple and sophisticated statistical techniques, which he calls "tools." The simple statistical tools are run charts, flow charts, fishbone charts, Pareto charts, histograms, and correlation charts. Surveys of customers are one of the most important tools because they tell a firm what to work on. According to Conway, these simple techniques can be used to solve 85 percent of a company's problems, while more complicated statistical process control methods are needed only about 15 percent of the time.

Furthermore, Conway points out that once a process is in control, the people responsible for it become more creative in eliminating variations because they know that they are personally capable of improving the system. In fact, people at the bottom make the most improvement because they learn "how to be logical all the time." Conway says this also applies to R & D operations, and since the United States is still the world leader in creativity and innovation, he is optimistic about its future.

Conway says it is possible to continually improve the productivity and quality performance of everyone in a firm on a monthly basis. "In less than one year, you ought to be able to perform miracles," he predicts. This miracle has already been performed by the Japanese, who have caused what Conway terms a "paradigm shift" in the way the world views quality. This shift is comparable to the discovery, centuries ago, that the earth was round.

In his talks, Conway does not dwell for long on purchasing or any other function because he believes his principles apply to all areas. Focusing efforts on one area is not sufficient to change the management "system" of a company. He says, however, that the creation and implementation of the new system is intended to be customized for each department. In fact, it is not necessary to wait for someone at the top to start the change; they can be shown by example the "right way to manage."

Conway's call for constant improvement in all areas of operations is intended to include a company's suppliers, and here, too, the key to success is the use of statistics. "It is just as vital to achieve statistical control of quality from your vendors as it is to have it internally," he says.

Overspecification, another form of waste in Conway's view, is not solely the responsibility of engineers. Purchasing managers and anyone connected with the design of a product are also responsible. He warns that specifications—like work standards—sometimes "cap" improvements.

In addition to working closely with clients, Conway Quality also provides training materials and furnishes a three-month implementation plan for management, called the "Gold Plan," which is a step-by-step plan for improving quality and productivity.

Conway's 6 Tools for Quality Improvement

1. Human relations skills—the responsibility of management to create at every level, among all employees, the motivation and training to make the necessary improvements in the organization.

2. Statistical surveys—the gathering of data about customers (internal as well as external), employees, technology, and equipment to be used as a measure for future progress and to identify what needs to be done.

3. Simple statistical techniques—clear charts and diagrams that help identify problems, track work flow, gauge progress, and indicate solutions.

4. Statistical process control—the statistical charting of a process, whether manufacturing or nonmanufacturing, to help identify and reduce variation.

5. Imagineering—a key concept in problem solving, involves the visualization of a process, procedure, or operation with all waste eliminated.

6. Industrial engineering—common techniques of pacing, work simplification, methods analysis, plant layout, and material handling to achieve improvements.

APPENDIX C

Foundation and Approach in Japan by

an Eminent Japanese Professor,

Kaoru Ishikawa

QC CIRCLE ACTIVITIES[1]

1.1 History of Industrial Development in Japan

The year 1968 marks the centennial anniversary of the Meiji Restoration. In 1868, 100 years ago, Emperor Meiji was enthroned and regained sovereignty of Japan. The year was made the first year of the Meiji Era. It was a memorable, epoch-making year for Japan that she started a new lease of life as a modern nation, a big shift from an agrarian economy and feudal social system dominated by the Tokugawa Bakufu and war-lords to a modern, industrial society.

Prior to the Meiji Era, industries were almost non-existent in Japan. To a limited extent cottage industries developed on a shoestring operation basis. The level of illiteracy was extremely high, resulting from an inadequate education system of the country under the feudalistic rule. The best one could do for schooling was to attend a cottage-scale classroom usually found in and conducted by a temple or shrine.

However, since the dawn of the Meiji Era the country-wide education system was developed and schools of differing levels of education in a range from the elementary school to the university were rapidly built in major cities, towns and villages the country over. The elementary school education was made compulsory by the law, with the result that the illiteracy rate was fast declining. At higher educational institutions such as universities, colleges, etc., however, the faculty members were mostly Westerners who had come from the U.S. and European countries and were doing teaching in technique and science. This condition continued for quite sometime, but was gradually recti-

---

1. Edited by Kaoru Ishikawa Union of Japanese Scientists & Engineers

fied when a number of Japanese educators gained mastery of Western studies and rose to the level of professorship. By 1900 the greater majority of professors in most universities were Japanese.

In the industrial sector, technology was introduced for the most part from foreign countries during those years in Meiji. Japanese scientists and engineers had competence enough to absorb and digest the newly introduced technology of the West and they played an instrumental role in the growth of industrialization in all branches of industry.

The Meiji Era ended in 1912 and the Taisho Era began thereafter. Japanese industry continued to grow over these years. World War I (1914–1919) in which Japan had no part sparked the rapid growth of her industry, for she was kept busy filling orders for war supplies from foreign countries. However, technology then used in industry was still "imported" one for the most part. Industry still relied heavily upon industrially advanced countries of the West for new knowledge and improved practices.

Between the beginning of the Showa Era which was the year 1926 and World War II, her industrial activity was considerably intensified and strengthened, keeping up with the rapidly progressing pace of Japan's expanded armament program. Most industrial establishments have grown up as defense industry to satisfy military requirements. They introduced in manufacturing not only the imported technology but also own technology which they had developed over time. Her exports also witnessed a steady growth in those years and products produced in Japan were making rapid inroads in overseas markets. However, in the prewar period Japanese goods had a bad reputation for cheapness, both in price and quality. Generally, products "made in Japan" had a poor quality image and received little customer's acceptance. Nevertheless, she had to promote an increased level of foreign trade so as to be able to import necessary raw materials required in her endeavor of industrial development.

The end of World War II witnessed a complete destruction of her industry. Her potentials of recovering the war devastation and getting back to normalcy seemed almost impossible in the early postwar years. But somehow or other she managed to rise on her feet once again and started intensifying activities in all sectors of industry. New knowledge, techniques and practices of management as well as production technology, in which, it was found, Japan lagged considerably behind the Western countries, were rapidly introduced in industry. The growth of industry has brought with it an increased level of exports and her export volume has been on a constant upward trend year after year. On the other hand, people receiving higher education are increasing in number. In the postwar period the scope of the compulsory education system was expanded to even include the junior high school education (3–year program) above and beyond the elementary schooling (6–year program). Moreover, in recent years about 60% of junior high school graduates are moving up into higher educational institutions (3–year senior high school program), and later into universities (4–year program). It is estimated that the number of university graduates entering business will soon exceed those who enter business upon finishing junior high school education. This has had a far-reaching effect of enhancing the quality standard of both operators and engineers working in industry continuously upward. Today, an increasing number of companies have developed their own technology and know-how which are built on the past technology imported here since as early as the Meiji Era from abroad or succeeded in improving them still further. There are some interests which even export such technology and know-how back to where they originally came from and to other developing countries under the licencing arrangement. Many enlightened businessmen and industrialists are intensifying research and development activity and increasing R & D expenditure every year, realizing the importance of developing own technology in both manufacturing and product fields. It is, however, discouraging to see that the foreign exchange paid out to foreign countries for importation of technology combined still exceed that of technology exportation from Japan in value.

It is no longer news that Japanese economy is growing. This explosive economic and industrial development which has been described by the world as a "miracle" can be demonstrated by her growing export performance in such product fields as transistor radio, TV set, camera, watch, textile, ship, steel, motorcycle, and bulldozer, which are winning the smashing customers' acceptance in overseas markets. Behind the scene of this spectacular export growth, one should not overlook an important role which the quality control practice in industry has played over the past 20 years. Today, the quality control, both concept and practice, is fast infiltrating in industries of big and small size, from light industries to heavy and highly-specialized industries, at differing levels of application and has become a continuing phase of management responsibilities.

As such, Japan has grown up as one of the leading industrialized countries of the world. However, in the recent years a new social phenomenon is taking place, which exerts serious impact upon her industrial development: a growing shortage of blue-collar workers, particularly of the young age bracket, largely due to the recent trend that they move up into higher educational institutions or that they are attracted more to the service and leisure industries. Another factor contributing to this is the wide-spread adoption of birth control in most families in the postwar period. On the other hand, the population in the old age classification are growing in number because of the remarkable progress in medical science and availability of good health medicines. In other words, the Japanese population has taken up on a structure which resembles an inverted pyramid. An ever-mounting shortage of labor supply in the young age classification, accelerated by the high rate of young students moving up into higher educational institutions such as senior high schools and universities, has tended to push the wage rate continuously upward at the rate of about 10% every year. Today, this condition has grown to the extent that the increased labor cost in industry can no longer be offset by the corresponding gains in productivity. The dual nature of structure, which was one of the major features of Japanese industrial formation, is also fast dissolving, as an increasing number of small industries are forced to introduce more mechanized and rational approach to business so as to overcome the mounting labor costs and to remain competitive in business. However, it should be noted that there are still a large number of marginal, inefficient small interests whose productivity is still low at the level. They are quickly dropping out of business or at the brink of business failure. The most recent report indicates that from 500 to 700 companies in the small industry classification are becoming bankrupt every month because of the lack of management competence and, above all, rapidly growing labor cost.

A Japanese enterprise has features which are uniquely identifiable and can be distinguished from those of its American or European counterpart. They shall be discussed next:

(1) Ratio of own capital to borrowed capital is low. Consequently, Japan is highly vulnerable to international competition resulting from the foreign capital liberalization program.

(2) Profit to sales ratio and profit to capital ratio are low.

(3) Management-labor relations are marked by paternalism under which an employee pledges lifelong employment with the company.

(4) Labor movement is characterized by the company unionism with no or little development of union organization by job or occupation.

(5) Generally, the wage level is still low, compared to the U.S. standard (about one-third), though it is constantly on an upward hike at the present time. When all fringe benefits paid out to a worker by the company are considered, his real earnings run near the current wage level in the European countries.

(6) Factory workers at the operation level are all homogeneous in both educational and social backgrounds. Recently, a greater number of factory workers are being taken over by those who have completed senior high school education.

(7) Dual-structure nature of industry formation as mentioned earlier.

The QC circle movement which is now beginning to be widely accepted in industry and becoming to be firmly established as the company-wide standard operating procedure is the logical development of our endeavor of breaking through the above-stated barriers which have confronted Japanese industry at large. Although it is not *the* solution to our multifold problem, it provides a clue to the solution—a clue which is considered workable and effective in our industrial settings.

1.2 Historical Development of Quality Control Practice in Japanese Industry*

Up until the end of World War II, i.e., before 1945, no or little attempt had been made by industry to put into practice the modern statistical methods of quality control. The introductory period of SQC as we know it today in Japan was 1946 through 1950. At first, the statistical methods of quality control were introduced here mainly from the U.S.A. through the U.S.A. occupation forces in Japan and some American educators and specialists working in the field of quality control including Dr. W. E. Deming. Books and literatures on more rational and scientific approaches to quality control became to be introduced in industry from abroad, particularly the U.S.A. On the other hand, the QC Research Group was organized within the frameworks of the Union of Japanese Scientists and Engineers (JUSE) since 1948 and started intensifying QC educational activity. The members of the group consist of university professors on engineering and science and engineers drawn from leading industrial firms in Japan. Since 1949 the JUSE has started as one of its major programs the so-called QC Basic Course which is to be implemented over a 6-month period for the benefit of interested industrial organizations.

---

*About quality control in Japan, three reports have been published: namely, "Quality Control in Japan," *Reports of Statistical Application Research*, Vol. 6, Special Issue (1959), JUSE, "Quality Control in Japan," *ibid.*, Vol. 10, No. 1 (1963), and "Recent Trend of Quality Control in Japan," *ibid.*, Vol. 12, No. 1 (1965). Concerning more details, please refer to them.

In July, 1949, the Industrial Standardization Law was enforced in Japan. Under the provisions of this law, companies which are successful in meeting the quality requirements concerning the application of SQC, as prescribed by the law, are permitted to use the JIS symbol on their products by authority of the Minister of International Trade and Industry. The Japanese Standards Association was also organized then and started to actively undertake QC studies on a broader front. It has succeeded in establishing about 35 Japanese Industrial Standards, drawing heavily on statistical quality control methods.

The years 1951–1954 were the growth period of SQC. The adoption of SQC was widespread among the first-class industrial establishments which were most receptive to the introduction of more improved practices of management. A number of lecture meetings, seminars and courses were held in major cities of Japan, inviting a wider participation of people from business and industrial houses. Books and magazines on statistical and mathematical QC methods were published in increasing volume. The Deming Prize and the Deming Application Prize in 1951, the Minister of International Trade and Industry Prize in 1953 and the Quality Control Literature Prize in 1954 were established, respectively. In the case of the Deming Application Prize, the companies rated excellent for the application of a statistical quality control system have been awarded prizes upon rigid scrutiny by the Deming Prize Committee every year.

In the course of this period, a big stride on SQC methods and application thereof in industry was made. It produced a great deal of benefits for industry in form of increased profit. However, there remained three defects which were left unanswered. They are:

(1) Too much trend toward application of statistical methods in industry, as it was carried to the extreme.

(2) Standardization was promoted but with somewhat too much formality.

(3) Top management people had a sentiment which was far from being "QC conscious," thus resulting in no or little support and understanding by the top management.

In 1954, Dr. J. M. Juran came to Japan from the U.S.A., and in his series of lectures before many groups of Japanese managers and engineers, he emphasized the point in his newer orientation of quality control, stating that quality control was an integral part of management, and that it had to be practiced in the total context of improvement management. His statement contributed greatly to the emergence of newer orientation of quality control, popularly called total quality control.

During the years 1955–1960, we experienced the period of total quality control growth which permeated throughout industry. The total quality control practice as we understand it in Japan is different from the generally accepted concept of TQC triggered by Dr. A. V. Feigenbaum. In our concept of TQC each and all people in the organization hierarchy in the range from the top managers down to workers at the rank-and-file level have exposure to statistical quality control knowledge and jointly participate in the upgrading of company-wide quality control practice.

Starting from 1956 a long series of quality control programs "on the air" designed for the QC education of the first line supervisors were broadcast over the Japan Shortwave Broadcasting Corporation's nationwide hookup, the first of the kind in the history of radio broadcasting. On the other hand, "the National Quality Month" was designated, starting from 1960, under which the month of November every year has been designated as the quality month and various QC events have begun to be staged in the course of this month. In addition, the "Q" flag and "Q" symbol were also adopted, whereby companies subscribing to the QC movement were encouraged to hoist the flag atop the factory building and post the posters on the wall inside the factory.

In 1961, we planned to publish a magazine called *Gemba To QC (Quality Control for the Foreman)* for a wider dissemination among people in the first-line supervisory classification and attempted to organize many "QC circles" at the workshop level in factories. Our attempts were quite rewarding and since then we have obtained a great deal of fruitful results. The December 1967 figures show that the number of subscribers to the magazine have increased to 42,000, and that there were about 12,000 QC circles officially registered with the JUSE and an estimate of 60,000 QC circles organized but not registered.

Through these activities, all QC circle members including both foremen and workers have learned the concept of QC and simple, basic statistical techniques for application in their day-to-day work and succeeded in solving by themselves many operation problems in their workshops. For example, in one company where there were 3,000 employees with about 200 QC circles organized, each circle succeeded in solving four problems on the average every year and brought about a total annual savings of $20,000 in way of cost reduction.

During this period, the quality standard of our products as well as the quality control practice in industry have made a remarkable stride. This is particularly true in the recent years. Time and efforts put in by all people concerned with quality control were extremely rewarding. Today, the quality control study is in the "boom" as more and more people participate in various QC courses and seminars sponsored by many institutions working in the field of management study and productivity.

People participating in and QC reports submitted to the All-Japan QC Conferences in November 1967 number as follows:

	Attendance	Reports
5th Annual QC Conference for Top Management	220	—
17th Annual QC Conference for Middle Management and QC Staff	1,600	70
6th Annual QC Conference for Foremen	2,500	272
5th Annual QC Conference for Consumers	500	—

QUALITY CONTROL PROGRAMS ON THE AIR

Example 1.
NHK Radio Broadcasting (Japan Broadcasting Corporation) 15 minutes, Mon. through Fri., July 15–Aug. 30, 1957. "Recent Management and Quality Control System."
Chapter 1. Quality and management: quality control; production procedure; in-company standardization; quality assurance.
Chapter 2. Quality control on raw material and parts received from outside sources: ordering; delivery and inventory control; quality control in subcontracting firms.
Chapter 3. Process control and quality assurance: inspection and process control; diagnosis for defective; operating losses; analysis of causes of defective; work shop control; inspection.
Chapter 4. Preventive maintenance: instrumentation control; production and test equipment control; jigs and tools control.
Chapter 5. How to implement a quality control plan: quality consciousness; education and training of quality control engineers and technicians; organization; quality control program.
Example 2.
NHK Radio Broadcasting 15 minutes, Mon. through Fri., Oct. 1–Dec. 28, 1962.
Chapter 1. Production of better quality products: what is "quality"?; meaning of "control"; relation of inspection to quality; standardization; how to put a quality control plan into action.
Chapter 2. Elimination of defectives: quality and its variance; purposes of collecting data; data processing; measure of frequency distribution; how to use data; Pareto chart; check sheet; causes and effects diagram (Ishikawa diagram); how to find out problems; investigations as to locating the assignable causes of defective products; what is defective?; elimination of defectives; application of statistical methods; significance test about averages; estimation of the population mean; estimation of the difference between two population means.
Chapter 3. How to control: procedures for process control; production on the basis of standardization; operation standards; quality control education and training; the needs for quality control education and training; the way to check; how to interpret and use control charts; corrective actions; what items should the supervisor check?

Chapter 4. The responsibilities of quality assurance: quality assurance and inspection; 100 percent inspection and sampling inspection; foreman's role of quality assurance; the relation between the foreman and the inspection section; self-inspection; inspection control; quality assurance and process control; application of quality data; actions on customer complaints.

Chapter 5. Improvement of quality standard: attitude for improvement of quality; ways to improve; discovering the problems; the study of problem solving; even at a job shop level improvements can be made; standard operating procedures and improvement; re-improvement; suggestion system; re-improvement; production of better quality products at lower quality cost.

Chapter 6. The role of the foreman: responsibilities of the foreman; the foreman and improvements; the foreman and control; the foreman is a company leader; the foreman's impression of QC performance; at factories.

Example 3.

NHK TV Broadcasting 30 minutes a week, every Tue., Aug.–Nov., 1960.

Chapter 1. What is good quality?
"   2. Collecting and analyzing data.
"   3. What is quality?
"   4. Improvement.
"   5. Process capability studies.
"   6. Quality control practice in subcontracting companies and receiving inspection.
"   7. Shop control.
"   8. New product development.
"   9. Quality design.
"   10. Quality assurance.
"   11. Customer-complaints disposition.
"   12. How to promote a quality control plan.

1.3 Factors Contributing to Rapid Growth of Quality Control Practice in Japanese Industry

Factors responsible for the rapid growth of QC practice in industry are numerous. Next, I should like to isolate and describe those that stand out among them as follows:

(1) *Generally prevalent enthusiasm for further education.* Needless to say, the rate of illiteracy in Japan is practically nil. Everyone in industry has acquired basic, general knowledge adequate enough to understand the quality control and develop himself for further progress. He is constantly motivated to further education above and beyond the call of the formal compulsory education (up to the junior high school education). This higher level of educational status of the workers makes it easier for a company to administer and conduct QC training programs for them, both on-the-job and off-the-job.

(2) *Availability of QC courses and seminars for participation.* There are a wide variety of QC training courses and seminars

offered by many organizations and institutions working in the field of management study and productivity for participation by anyone, in a range from a short course to a long course, from the basic to the advanced. The JUSE alone has a cumulative total of about 30,000 alumni who have completed QC long-term and short-term seminars for various trainees over the last 19 years. Moreover, an increasing number of companies are developing and installing own QC training courses for not only people at the operation level but also people in the top management.

(3) *Invitation of top-level foreign educators to Japan provided a stimulus to the growth of interest in QC.* We have invited to Japan some world-renowned scholars and educators from abroad, including Dr. Deming and Dr. Juran, to have them conduct QC seminars before many groups of Japanese businessmen and industrialists, which have resulted in enhancing an increased level of interest in and concern with quality control. Their presence in Japan and contribution to industry in the form of QC education had a tremendous impact upon the progress of QC practice in industry.

(4) *Quality control practice adapted to our specific needs in industry established.* Over time we have developed our own quality control, both concept and practice, adapted to our specific requirements in industry and socio-cultural value system, which identifies itself as uniquely Japanese.

(5) *JIS (Japanese Industrial Standard) symbol and Deming Application Prize have become institutionalized.* Under the provision of the Japanese Industrial Standardization Law, companies desiring to have the JIS symbol printed on their products are required to submit themselves to examination with respect to the product quality and the quality control system by the concerned governmental agency for approval, whereas the Deming Application Prize is to be awarded to the companies which have excelled all others in the performance of quality control in that year. In each case, it involves a vast ground, preparatory work for companies running for candidates in setting up QC works in excellent order so as to be ready for taking the examination.

(6) *System of quality control audit by top management.* More and more companies are adopting the system of quality control audit by top management under which the quality of products produced and the QC system in operation are carefully

examined as a continuing phase of management responsibilities. It is generally practiced that such audit is made once or twice a year, dependent upon the specific requirements of each company, by visiting factories or business offices. Practice such as this produces effective results in that every one in the organization from the top to the bottom begins to have the awareness of importance and interest in quality control.

(7) *The National Quality Month has become to be firmly established.* As mentioned earlier, the National Quality Month which started from 1960 are being faithfully observed in November every year all over the country. In the course of this month, various QC programs and events take place in industry to renew people's determination of promoting the awareness of the importance of QC.

(8) *Increasingly important role of the first-line supervisors in QC.* It is quite evident that an effective groundwork of quality control can be accomplished largely in each workshop with a foreman at its nucleus. Unless the foreman in close collaboration with his workers put forth everything they have in implementing good quality control and assume full responsibility therefor, nothing much can be done in way of QC. With a view to strengthening the position of people at the operation level, there is an increasing trend in industry toward organizing a number of QC circles with a foreman at the nucleus of each circle to perform a linking function. Incidently, starting from 1962 a magazine titled *Quality Control for the Foreman* has become to be published for subscription by a large number of people in first-line supervisory classification. The subscription is increasing in circulation every year and the magazine is receiving a widespread readers' acceptance.

(9) *Export inspection system in Japan helps promote an increased standard of product quality.* By law, some kinds of products to be exported to overseas markets must be subjected to the governmental or independent institutions' inspection in order to insure a certain degree of quality assurance. This system, undoubtedly, is conducive to the overall upgrading of product quality and considered instrumental to an increasing interest in quality control in industry. But, these are some unresolved problems in administration.

(10) *Impacts of free competition and recent government's embarcation on foreign trade and capital liberalization.* The shift to the buyers' market from the sellers' market which had disappeared a

long time ago under the pressure of free competition has made it mandatory for many manufacturers to produce products of better quality at lower price, if they hope to stay in business and remain competitive. Under the concept "the customers are always right" or "the customers are king", the general buying public now have choice over a wide variety of products offered to markets by producers and are in a position to exert influence over the quality of products. The buyers have a wide latitude of freedom to choose from among many specific products or "brands" of specific quality. This condition was made much severer with the recent government's embarcation on the foreign trade and capital liberalization program. Regardless of whether it likes or not, Japanese industry has plunged into an era of free trade and free competition on an international basis. Confronted by the new challenge, the management of most companies are seriously tackling the problem of quality control and intensifying activities which help strengthen their system of quality control by introducing new methods, different approaches, and improved practices developing in the field of management science.

1.4 Characteristics of Japanese Quality Control

As history, culture, language, etc. vary from country to country, the treatment of quality control likewise varies, dependent upon the situational requirements of the country. Since the early dawn of the Meiji Era Japan has taken in new knowledge and technology from abroad and digested them over time in such a way that she has succeeded in developing own technology building on the past knowledge and experience. A similar process was also true of her establishing own quality control, both theory and practice, which is tailored to the specific needs of the country. She continues to capitalize on new knowledge in management and science developing in Japan and abroad to establish a still newer and better quality control system. Let me attempt to describe next the outstanding characteristics of the quality control practiced in Japanese industry over the last 10 years, with all its strength and weakness considered:

(1) Quality control is not limited to one functional area of management merely attended to by QC engineers. It is a company-wide treatment in which all people from the top managers down to the rank-and-filers, from design department through purchasing department to sales department, participate in a highly organized fashion.

(2) Statistical methods are popularly used in each workshop. In so far as the utilization in industry of statistical methods including design of experiments is concerned, Japan probably gets far ahead of other nations.

(3) The level of QC education is quite high in industry. Most companies administer and implement in-company QC courses for the employees and/or encourage them to participate in QC courses and seminars sponsored by outside organizations.

(4) Top managers actively participate in QC audit of the company.

(5) The system of new product development is integrated with and superimposed on that of quality control.

(6) The quality level targetted heretofore by industry has been world first-class quality towards which many progressive companies have striven to upgrade the product quality. Most recently, some of them have achieved or surpassed the level and are now in the process of achieving the quality level which is considered the world best. Those marginal, inefficient companies which produce products of inferior quality are gradually disappearing from the scene of business because of inability to effectively compete with others in markets.

(7) There are some groups, consisting of educators, specialists and engineers, which have continuously been promoting statistical quality control and its applications in industry. Most typical is the QC Research Group organized in the JUSE working in the past two decades.

(8) These groups are performing a linkage function between statisticians, men of theory, and engineers, men of action, to constantly upgrade quality control practice in industry.

(9) Establishment of the Deming Application Prize for quality control and the Prize of the Minister of International Trade and Industry for standardization has helped promote an increased level of interest in and awareness of the importance of quality control, as mentioned earlier.

(10) QC is interpreted in a broader sense of the term in industry. In our orientation we use it in a broadly-stretched concept which includes all improvement management activities that permeate throughout the organization or the system. It is not necessarily limited to one functional area of management.

(11)   It is generally accepted practice in industry that we even treat reliability as an integral part of quality assurance. Recently, the level of quality assurance has made a remarkable stride, but it is still far from being adequate and satisfactory.

QUALITY CONTROL SYSTEM IN JAPAN[2]

1. Introduction

Recently, a number of Japanese products are winning reputations as the results and fruits of the quality control efforts applied over the past 20 years.

But, in Japan we have some problems. Every year, employees have 15–20% raise of the wage base, so we must make better quality and higher price products continuously, that is we must produce the best quality in the world and increase labor productivity. For example, in 1972 the exports of black and white television sets from Taiwan are larger than those from Japan.

The second problem is Dollar's shocks. After the Nixon's shock or Dollar's shock in August 1971 and the revaluation of yen in December 1971 (from 360 to 308 yen/dollar), there are two evident tendencies. If some products had been exported because of good quality, after the shock, the prices rose and the quantities of export did not decrease, but those products because of cheap prices the quantities decreased. After the second revaluation (now floating) of yen and the devaluation of dollar in February 1973 (from 308 to 260. 70 yen/dollar), we must produce still much better quality and still cheaper cost products. So, hereafter, we should apply more intensive quality control system, export higher quality level industrial products and import lower quality level industrial products and raw materials.

2. History of QC in Japan

Before and during World War II, (i.e., before 1945), we had little application of modern and statistical quality control.

The introductory period was during 1946–1950. At first, SQC was introduced from the U.S., by, for example, the U.S. Army, Dr. W. E. Deming (USA), and many books. Since 1948, QC Research Group was started at the Union of Japanese Scientists and Engineers

---

2. Dr. Kaoru Ishikawa, University of Tokyo—Japan

(JUSE). The members of this group were professors of engineering and statistics, government officers, and engineers from private companies. Since 1949, JUSE has begun a long lecture QC seminar, so-called the QC Basic Course. The Industrial Standardization Law was enforced in July, 1949, and in this law a system was decided upon to present the JIS certification mark on some commercial goods by authorization of the Minister of International Trade and Industry. The Japanese Standards Association (JSA) also began to hold research meetings in QC methods, and since then has established about 37 Japanese Industrial Standards for Statistical Quality Control. In 1950, we started to publish the magazine "Statistical Quality Control" (JUSE) and "Standardization and Quality Control" (JSA).

The years 1951–1954 were the years of development of SQC. The Deming Prize and the Deming Prize for Application in 1951, the Minister of International Trade and Industry Prize in 1953, and the QC Literature Prize in 1954 were established.

In this period, QC and statistical method progressed and we achieved many good results although there remained three defects:

(a) There was too much tendency towards statistical methods.

(b) Standardization was promoted but with somewhat too much formality.

(c) QC was far from top management.

At that time, in 1954, Dr. J. M. Juran (USA) came to Japan and emphasized that QC should be conducted as an integral part of management control.

Between the years 1955–1960, we have been going through what might be called the permeation period of Company-Wide Quality Control (CWQC). In Japan, when one company wants to apply CWQC, all the employees, from the top management to the foremen and workers, study statistical methods and participate in QC.

"National Quality Month" started in 1960, and since has been observed every November, and the "Q" flag and "Q" mark were established.

("Q" Mark)

In 1962, we planned to publish a magazine called "GEMBATO-QC" (QC for the Foreman) and to organize "QC Circle" in workshops of various factories.

International Conference on Quality Control (ICQC '69–Tokyo) was held October 1969 in Tokyo under the sponsorship of JUSE in cooperation with the American Society for Quality Control (ASQC) and the European Organization for Quality Control (EOQC), and under the consensus of Six Man Board of International Academy for Quality (IAQ). This was the first international conference on quality control recognized as the worldwide scale. The conference theme was "the world prosperity through quality!" From 44 countries, there were 1,067 attendants and 233 papers were contributed.

3. Differences in QC between Japan and Western Countries

Each country has its different background, such as different cultural patterns, different religions, different languages, different historical development, different educational development, different mobility of labor, different labor union system, different professional system, and different political regime. It may be a mono-race nation or multi-race nation. These differences are reflected in the way of executing quality control.

Differences in QC between Japan and western countries are as follows.

1) In Japan, QC education and QC training are commonly available to people of all levels, from the top management to the bottom workers. In the West, QC tends to be available only to QC engineers. On the contrary, in Japan, the top management and the workers are all involved in QC system and every one in the company participates and executes QC.

2) In Japan, statistical methods are commonly known by not only QC engineers, but also all company personnel from the top management to the workers through education. So they can practically use SQC methods.

3) Our QC Circles, which consist of workers and foremen, and their activities are far superior in the world; many western countries take now interest in the QC Circle activities. But, through my experiences, I would like to say, in other countries except Chinese letter countries, (i.e., China and Korea), it will be impossible to apply just same QC Circle activities, because they have different background. They must develop their modified QC Circle activities.

4) Japan has not enough established a functional system for quality assurance on a company basis.

5) Government does not force quality control. However each company voluntarily adopted QC. This is one of the good points of free competition and free foreign trade. QC will be most effectively developed under free competition, free foreign trade, and democratic industrial organization.

4. Six Features of Quality Control in Japan

4.1 Company-wide QC—CWQC   QC in Japan is characterized by company-wide participation, from the top management to the employees. It is an activity participated in by not only the departments of technology, design, research and manufacturing but also sales, materials and clerical or management departments such as planning, accounting, business, and personnel.

QC concepts and methods are used for solving troubles in the production process, for incoming material control and new product development control, and also for making business analyses when the top management decides on a company policy, and for solving problems in the clerical departments.

4.2 QC Audit   (1) QC Audit by the Top Management

The QC Audit is carried out by the top management of the company and in another means of promoting company-wide QC in Japan. An audit team of executives headed by the president of the company visits each plant, sales office, and department to investigate the degree to which the company policy and the promotion of QC programs are being carried out and eliminates any obstacle which might hinder their activities.

(2) The Deming Prize for Application

The Deming Prize was established to commemorate the friendship and achievements of Dr. W. E. Deming. It is actually two prizes: the Deming Prize and the Prize for Application. They are awarded to individuals or companies after examination by the Deming Prize Committee. It is very important that this committee is not governmental committee and there are no economical award and no certification mark.

(3) JIS (Japanese Industrial Standard) Certification Mark

There are 36 Japanese Industrial Standards for control charts, sampling inspection, and design of experiments and they are contributing to the nationwide dissemination of QC.

The "JIS" mark gives a national guarantee of quality to Japanese products. All good products bear the "JIS" mark, whether they come from small, middle, or large enterprises. To be eligible for "JIS" approval, a company must practice SQC. The "JIS" mark may be given only after this condition is satisfied, and after investigation on the state of SQC application. For plants with superior JIS application rating, there are other awards, such as the Minister of International Trade and Industry Prize, the Institute of Industry and Technology Prize, and the MITI Regional Bureau Prize.

4.3 Industrial Education and Training   Historically, Japan has always been keen on education. Literacy is over 99%, with 99% of the people graduating from middle school, 86% from high school, and 27% from college or university.

As for QC education, a remarkable amount of education has been carried out from 1949, both inside and outside the company and from the top management to the workers. QC Circle activities are also an asset in this training.

4.4 QC Circle Activities   One major characteristic of Japanese company-wide QC is the QC Circle movement started in 1962. In 1961, we planned to publish a magazine called "GEMBA-TO-QC" (QC for the Foreman) and to organize many QC Circles. This enables the low level employees, (i.e. foremen and workers), in a workshop, clerks or salesmen in branch office to carry out QC activities voluntarily and through self- and mutual-development.

4.5 Application of Statistical Methods   The application of statistical methods is one of the pillars of Japanese QC. Its characteristics are the following three:

1) Statistical methods are used by a wide range of persons, from the top to the bottom of the company.

2) Statistical Methods are used extensively in the company. Statistical methods are applied in every department (e.g., technology, production, testing planning, purchasing, warehouses, sales, accounting, personnel, and general affairs).

3) The level of the statistical methods used is high.

4.6 Nationwide QC Promotion Activities   In Japan the core of QC promotion is made up of private organizations such as JUSE (Union of Japanese Scientists and Engineers) and JSA (Japanese Standards Association) rather than governmental QC promotion activities.

In November every year, various events are held to observe "Quality Month," sponsored by these organizations, or under joint sponsorship with related organizations and with the support of the government Ministries. The events of this month are part of the Nationwide QC promotion activities. Besides the following events, some booklets (7 kinds in 1971) are published.

Events (1971)	Attendance	Started
• 9th QC Annual Conference for Top Management	200	1963
•11th QC Annual Conference for QC Staff and Middle Management	1,500	1951
•10th QC Annual Conference for the Foreman	2,500	1962
• 9th QC Annual Conference for Consumers	200	1963
•21st QC Annual Public Lecture Meetings	4,000	—

Furthermore, QC Circle Meetings are held about 60 times a year all over the country. The number of persons attending these conferences and meetings in 1972 was 50,000. At these occasions, presentations of QC research and reports of application activities are given, and discussions and plant tours are held.

In every October, we have "Standardization Promotion Month," and the Standardization National Conference is held.

5. Quality Control and Government in Japan

Each company should adopt quality control voluntarily. If the government force quality control and most of the governmental QC specialists, have only SQC concept and methods on the desk and papers, and they have a little experiences in practice, QC easily becomes a formal QC or documental QC.

The relationships of quality control and the Japanese government are as follows, but most of the companies adopted quality control voluntarily through private organizations and volunteers and the impetuses by the government.

5.1 The impetuses by the government The impetuses by the government are very important to promote quality control in private companies.

1) *The system of free competition and free trade.* It is elementary that if goods are scarce or production is monopolistic, even bad products can be sold in the resulting seller's market. However, if competition prevails and goods are in sufficient supply, the choice of consumers will come strong, making the quality of

products and the quality control in industries more and more important. Just after the war, the Japanese market was a seller's market. In free competition and free trade, the market is a buyer's market. Since then, the Japanese industries, especially the top management, have made good efforts to develop quality controls voluntarily which are adequate for free competition and free trade, to turn out good quality products and offer them at optimum price. Restriction of imports is only a passive strategy, to a favorable trade balance. We have chosen to adopt a more positive strategy, that is to free foreign trade gradually.

2) *The depression policy.* After the War II, we met several times depressions in various kind of companies. In Japan fortunately, politician, government officers, and economists did not know how to avoid depression in the system of free competition. In the case of depression, some of the managements enthusiastically promoted their quality control programs.

5.2 JIS certification mark   One of the key characteristics of the Japanese Industrial Standardization Law is a provision for the enforcement of a system to identify standard products. The companies are requested to apply statistical quality control and to pass an examination of the company's quality control system by the Japanese government, before they are entitled to stamp the JIS certification mark on their products. The JIS mark systems have prompted SQC and have worked out as a good impetus, but there are some formidable problems in administering these audits properly.

However, fortunately, the Japanese government does not force the JIS mark. If the quality level of the product of a company is extremely higher than JIS quality level, and if the top management want to put his company's brand, they will put the company's brand instead of the JIS mark.

5.3 Export Inspection Acts   In Japan, in 1957 we established Export Inspection General Law to prevent exporting low quality level products, and we have now 38 kinds of export inspection acts. At first, these systems were effective to prevent exporting poor quality goods from the vicious producers and through vicious foreign buyers and domestic merchants. But recently most of the Japanese products are better than inspection levels, so these systems are not so effective.

5.4 QC Audit by the government   In Japan, some of governments and public corporation (such as Defense Agency and Nippon Telegraph and Telephone Public Corporation) audit the quality control systems of suppliers.

As the above, in Japan Quality Control has something to do with government. Though, QC will become a formal QC, if auditors, who are QC specialists in the government, have not enough experiences to execute QC practice. So, I often give advice to the suppliers as follows: "Never sit for the QC audit to pass the examination, on the contrary, you must sit to promote your company's quality control through QC audit."

6. Nationwide Quality Control Promotion System

In Japan, we have not a professional organization, such as the American Society for Quality Control and the European Organization for Quality Control. In 1971, we established the Japanese Society for Quality Control (JSQC) but this society is only an academic society and not a professional society.

Most of the nationwide quality control promotion activities have been propelled through private organization (JUSE, the Committee for QC Annual Conferences and the Committee for Quality Month), and public organization (JSA). The members of the both Committees for QC Annual Conference and Quality Month are volunteers from QC research group, who want to propel QC in Japan. JUSE and JSA back up these two committees, but financially committees are managed on the self-paying basis. The Committee for QC Annual Conferences plans and manages four annual conferences, for Top Management, for QC Staff and Middle Management, for Foreman, and for Consumers and QC Annual Public Lecture Meetings, which are held in every November.

In the case of QC Circle Activities, we established QC Circle Headquarters in JUSE. The Organization to promote QC Circle Activities is as follows:

QC Circle Headquarters
    President: The chairman of the board of director of JUSE
    Executive Directors: The chairman and two vice chairmen of Editorial Board of GEMBA-TO-QC (FQC)
    Advisors: The members of Editorial Board of FQC
    Honorary Advisors: The advisors for Editorial Board of FQC
    Secretariat: JUSE
We have now seven Regional Headquarters of QC Circle, from Hokkaido to Kyushu.

Regional Chairman: Director of private company
Regional Vice Chairman (Chairman Elect): Director of private company
Regional Executive Secretary: QC staff of chair company
Secretaries: QC staffs and foremen of private companies
Advisor: One of the members of Editorial Board of FQC

Recently, we established section systems under the Regional Headquarters. In the case of Kanto Regional Headquarters, it has seven sections. The organization of section is just same as regional headquarters.

All of the officers of QC Circle Headquarters are persons in private companies and professors, and no governmental officers. They serve on QC Circle promotion activities passionately with almost no pay.

APPENDIX D

The Malcolm Baldrige National Quality Award by

the Department of Commerce Director

THE MALCOLM BALDRIGE NATIONAL QUALITY AWARD

Introduction

Over the past decade, the U.S. has experienced a decline in its balance of trade. Though many factors contribute to this trend, evidence is mounting that quality—real and perceived—of U.S. goods is one of the significant factors. Surveys show that buyers are becoming more quality conscious, and that in the minds of some, "made in America" is no longer a symbol of quality.

The growing concern over quality, particularly as it related to U.S. competitiveness, led some members of Congress and the Administration to consider options for raising awareness of quality. One of the mechanisms considered was a national quality award for businesses, akin to Japan's Deming Prize, which is widely credited with having played a major role in reversing Japan's earlier reputation for poor quality.

In the mid 1980's, some members of Congress became interested in the quality issue, stimulated in part by John J. Hudiburg, Chairman of the Florida Power and Light Company. In 1986, legislation was introduced to create a national award. In 1987, following the accidental death of Secretary of Commerce, Malcolm Baldrige, the national award legislation, then pending, was named for Mr. Baldrige, and the legislation quickly passed both Houses of Congress. President Reagan signed the Malcolm Baldrige National Quality Improvement Act of 1987 (P.L. 100–107) into law on August 20, 1987.

Responsibility for the Malcolm Baldrige Award was assigned to the Department of Commerce. The National Institute of Standards and Technology (NIST), an agency of the Department of Commerce, was given responsibility for the development and management of the Award Program.

KEY PROVISIONS OF THE MALCOLM BALDRIGE NATIONAL QUALITY IMPROVEMENT ACT

The Malcolm Baldrige National Quality Improvement Act of 1987 sets certain specific requirements for the Award and for the management of the Award Program. Requirements include:

- *Categories for Award*: 1) manufacturing companies or subsidiaries; 2) service companies or subsidiaries; and 3) small business. Up to two awards may be given each year in each category.

- *Criteria for Qualification*: Apply in writing to the Director of NIST, and permit rigorous evaluation.

- *Awards*: A medal bearing the inscription "Malcolm Baldrige National Quality Award" presented by the President or the Secretary of Commerce. Award recipients may publicize and advertise based upon receipt of the Award.

- *Award Examination*: NIST shall rely upon a Board of Examiners to conduct reviews and site visits.

- *Technology Transfer*: The NIST Director shall ensure feedback to applicants and publicize successful quality improvement strategies.

- *Award Program Oversight*: The Secretary of Commerce shall appoint a prestigious Board of Overseers to review Award processes and suggest improvement.

- *Funding*: The Secretary of Commerce is authorized to seek and accept gifts and to impose fees upon applicants.

In summary, these requirements show that awards are to be made to companies for excellence of quality management and achievement as judged through detailed evaluations made by peers. Development and operating costs are to be borne by the private sector. The government's primary roles are creating, validating, and improving Award processes and ensuring effective technology and information transfer.

Design Features

The Law sets a number of key requirements for the U.S. national quality award, but nevertheless affords considerable latitude in Award criteria and processes.

To ensure a broad base of input to the design of the Award, many quality leaders—manufacturing, service, academic, consultants, and retired—were contacted regarding characteristics that should be incorporated into the award. The requirements specified in the law and the advice of quality leaders were synthesized into a "value system" for the Award. Key elements of the value system are as follows:

1. Total Quality Management. The Award should stress total quality control—all operations and functions. This should include integration of quality planning with business planning.

2. Human Resource Utilization. The Award should emphasize training and development of all personnel with particular stress on quality training.

3. Performance. The Award should be heavily performance based. That is, it should give considerable weight to quality improvement results, in preference to specific techniques or processes for achieving results.

4. "Measurables". Award criteria and application evaluation should focus on quantitative results and positive trends, rather than on narrative descriptions of processes and anecdotal information. To be in a position to respond convincingly, firms would have to have in place a good quality measurement system, along with associated analytical capabilities.

5. Customer Satisfaction. The Award criteria should give major consideration not only to customers' views of products and services, but also to the functioning of the entire customer interface in planning products and services.

6. World-Class Quality. Award evaluation should, where appropriate, explore the degree to which firms recognize the quality requirements of international markets, their systems for assessing where they stand, and their plans for establishing a leadership position.

7. Quality Early in the Process. Award criteria should reflect the need to address quality early in the design phase, both to reduce delays in bringing products to market and to enter markets with higher-quality products.

8. Innovation. Award application should permit firms to highlight and get credit for unique approaches to achieving higher quality.

9. External Leadership. Award evaluations should give some weight to applicants' efforts to lead and support national and local activities in support of quality and its related infrastructure. This includes assisting suppliers, supporting quality standards, creating community councils, etc.

STRATEGIC DESIGN

The Award Program has been strategically designed to achieve *all* of the aims of the legislation as well as those of the quality community. It is also designed to minimize the problems inherent in setting up a program which involves many people with different quality expertise, viewpoints, and organizational ties. Though the design strategy involves many facets, there are four key elements of the design:

Criteria The Award value system has been embodied in criteria organized into seven categories. This was done to convey the meaning of a total quality control system that would be useful for businesses whether or not they apply for an award. Each category probes areas of quality management that are most likely to reveal characteristics of excellent companies. The categories provide a balance between "process" and "results", and adapt to differing definitions of quality. Criteria are written to minimize the distinctions between manufacturing and services so that one examination may be used for all businesses.

Scoring System The scoring system—created for the Award Program—is designed to provide high resolution at the upper end of the scale, suitable for distinguishing characteristics of the excellent companies expected to apply for Awards. The system is "three dimensional"—based upon approach, extent of deployment, and results. The scoring system and the scoring method are integrated, and form the basis not only for evaluation but also for providing feedback to applicants.

Evaluation Process The evaluation is built around multiple, independent review, followed by a consensus process. High-scoring applicants are site visited for further evaluation. Award recipients are recommended by a Panel of Judges who use scoring information and site visit reports to make their judgments.

The evaluation process is designed to minimize the effects of variability in scoring and potential conflicts of interest. This process also recognizes the need for a balance between scoring and judgment owing to many factors including the need to have Award recipients serve as national models.

Organizational Structure The organizational structure is designed to ensure the integrity of Award processes and to help promote information transfer. Since some organizations provide funding, and other groups evaluate and advise, the organization must ensure proper separation of functions. Since many organizations in the U.S. participate in or have a stake in quality improvement activities, the Award organization needs to permit easy access to the Award and to Award results.

AWARD ORGANIZATION

The Award organization was designed to carry out the specific responsibilities spelled out in the Law as well as to facilitate the larger purposes—information transfer and quality awareness—that motivated the creation of the Law. Through formal and informal linkages among new and existing organizations, the Award organization serves as a vehicle for quality awareness involving many people and organizations in the Award Program and for information transfer. The Award organization is shown in Figure 1.

Department of Commerce   The Department of Commerce is the Federal Department assigned responsibility for the basic directions of the Award Program. The Secretary of Commerce, together with the President, present the Awards.

National Institute of Standards and Technology (NIST)   NIST, an agency of the Department of Commerce, is assigned day-to-day pro-

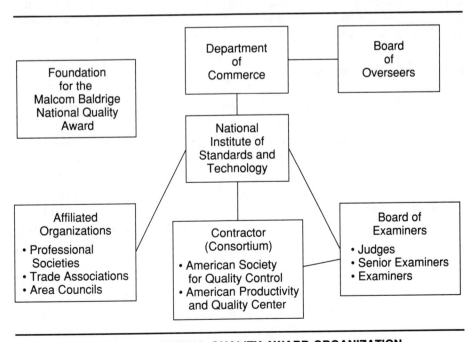

FIGURE 1.   NATIONAL QUALITY AWARD ORGANIZATION

gram management of the Award Program. Responsibilities include creation of Award criteria and processes, staffing of Boards, contract monitoring, feedback to applicants, and information transfer.

Contractor   The Contractor is a consortium of the American Society for Quality Control and the American Productivity and Quality Center. The contractor carries out a number of operations of the Award Program such as management of the application review, preparation of promotional materials, and assistance with publicity.

Board of Overseers   The Board of Overseers, appointed by the Secretary of Commerce, advises the Secretary and the Director of NIST on broad directions of the Award Program. The recommendations of the Board will guide the evolution of the Award Program so that it best serve the national interest.

Board of Examiners   The Board of Examiners, appointed by the Director of NIST, consists of quality experts selected on the basis of expertise, experience, and peer recognition. Beginning in September 1987, NIST began networking with a variety of organizations and individuals to identify leaders who could take part in the review process. An examiner application was developed jointly by NIST and the Consortium. Application materials include information on terms and conditions of involvement, compensation, and a code of ethics. There were more than 300 applicants and referrals for the Board of Examiners. The Board for 1989 consists of 134 examiners, all meeting very high standards of qualification.

Examiner Preparation   All examiners take part in a three-day preparation course. The course focuses on understanding of criteria, scoring system, evaluation process, and on developing consensus evaluations. Case studies developed for the preparation courses are used as the principal means to orient the examination team. The main emphasis throughout the courses is reducing variability in scoring.

In order to maintain a team identity among examiners and to keep examiners informed of developments in the Award Program, a newsletter called *Update* was created.

Foundation   P.L. 100–107 authorizes the Secretary of Commerce to seek and accept gifts to support the Award Program. Secretary of Commerce, C. William Verity, invited Mr. John Hudiburg, CEO of the Florida Power and Light Company, and Mr. Sanford McDonnell, Chairman Emeritus of the McDonnell Douglas Corporation, both strong supporters of the national quality award concept, to organize the Foundation for the Malcolm Baldrige National Quality Award. The Foundation would need to be entirely independent of both the government and the organizations that conduct application review and program oversight. As of June 30, 1989, the Foundation is led by 44 senior business executives; more than $10.4M has been pledged to date. A memorandum of agreement has been established between the Foundation and NIST through which funds are made available to the contractor, with contract monitoring carried out by NIST.

Affiliates   Many organizations in the U.S.—trade associations, professional societies, area councils, etc.—have a stake in quality improvement in the U.S. Most of these organizations have members who could participate in some way in the Award Program. All such organizations could play a major role in information transfer.

The principal purpose of the Affiliates Program will be to create a vehicle to make available the Award findings for use in education and training programs throughout the United States. This approach is being taken because NIST does not wish to duplicate any of the many excellent programs now available. Rather, it seeks to strengthen these programs through encouraging the incorporation of the unique findings of the Award Program. Cooperative workshops, symposia, and publications will be developed among affiliates according to need and opportunity.

AWARD CRITERIA AND PROCESSES

The Award is based upon well-defined criteria spelled out in detail in the application guidelines. The criteria are organized into seven categories as follows:

Leadership: The senior management's success in creating and sustaining a quality culture. (12 percent weight)

Information and Analysis: The effectiveness of the company's collection and analysis of information for quality improvement and planning. (6 percent weight)

Planning: The effectiveness of integration of quality requirements into the company's business plans. (8 percent weight)

Human Resource Utilization: The success of the company's efforts to utilize the full potential of the work force for quality. (15 percent weight)

Quality Assurance: The effectiveness of the company's systems for assuring quality control of all operations. (14 percent weight)

Quality Assurance Results: The company's results in quality achievement and quality improvement, demonstrated through quantitative measures. (15 percent weight)

Customer Satisfaction: The effectiveness of the company's systems to determine customer requirements and demonstrated success in meeting them. (30 percent weight)

The dynamic relationships among the Award categories are shown in Figure 2.

In the 1989 examination, applicants were required to address 44 examination items. They were instructed to provide factual information, data, and trends to demonstrate both continued progress and high levels of success. While these criteria cover the process by which companies address quality, the emphasis of the Award and the challenge to applicants is on the achievement of quality, as indicated by the high weight placed on results and customer satisfaction.

APPLICATION REVIEW

In 1989, a first-stage review process was introduced based upon scoring of sixteen "indicator items" representing the key areas in the seven examination categories. Because of its first time use, scoring of the sixteen items was carried out independently by six examiners. Applicants scoring approximately in the upper one-half of the applicant pool were referred for consensus review.

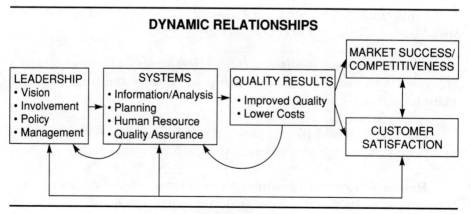

DYNAMIC RELATIONSHIPS

FIGURE 2

Consensus review begins with the assignment of each application to three examiners and a senior examiner. (Assignments are made taking into account potential conflicts of interest.) The four team members independently score an application based upon a scoring system developed for the Award Program and reviewed and practiced on case studies in examiner preparation courses. Scores and comments on strengths, areas for improvement, and site visit issues are given for each of the examination items. Examiners then forward their scores to a senior examiner who develops a consensus score for each item and an aggregated list of comments and site visit issues. Attaining consensus requires consultation among examiners to make certain that the entire team contributes to the resolution of differences in scoring.

Based upon the consensus scores, the Judges Panel decides for or against a site visit. This decision—based not only upon the scores of an applicant but also upon the scores of *all* applicants—ensures that site visits will be made to all applicants that should be considered in the final Award recommendation process. The written evaluation process is shown schematically in Figure 3.

If an applicant is selected for a site visit, the company is notified and the site visit team prepares for the visit. Site visit issues are translated into a specific visit agenda, with each member of the 3 or 4 member site visit team given a specific assignment. The site visit team meets just prior to the visit to make certain of all plans. While visiting, members of the team "caucus" periodically to review findings and to make midcourse corrections, if necessary. Upon completion of the visit, the team prepares a summary report of its findings. The stages of a site visit examination are shown schematically in Figure 4.

Site visit reports, consensus scores, and examiner comments are forwarded to the Judges Panel for final recommendations. The Judges

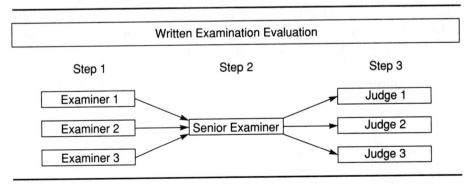

FIGURE 3

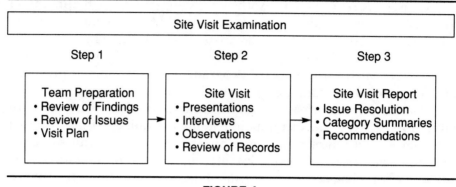

FIGURE 4

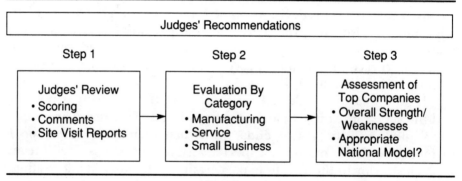

FIGURE 5

review all information on the remaining applicants and then evaluate these applicants one by one by category. This step usually involves interviews with the senior examiners who led the site visits. As each application is considered, Judges with conflicts of interest are excluded from the discussion (at no time during the review cycle do Judges with conflicts of interest take part in or receive information relative to applications for which they are excluded). After the final two candidates have been selected in a category, the Judges evaluate against an "absolute" standard—the overall excellence of the company in the seven award examination categories. The stages of the Judges' evaluation are shown schematically in Figure 5.

1988 AWARD PROGRAM

Sixty-six companies applied for Awards. By category, the applicants were distributed as follows:

- manufacturing — 45
- services — 9
- small businesses — 12

Of these applicants, thirty-two are entire companies; thirty-four are subsidiaries or divisions of larger companies. All twelve of the small businesses are whole companies. Among the manufacturing and service companies, twenty of the fifty-four applicants are whole companies.

Applications were evaluated using the procedures described above. In the consensus review, each examiner spent an average of about sixteen hours to score and develop comments. Senior examiners spent an average of about eighteen hours to review the work of examiners, and to develop consensus scores and comments.

Based upon overall scoring and examination team comments, thirteen companies were selected for site visits. By category, the companies site visited were as follows:

- manufacturing — 10
- services — 2
- small businesses — 1

Visits were conducted in accordance with the procedures described above. Summary reports were developed for each visit. These reports included information on the resolution of issues raised in the review of written applications and comments on overall strengths and areas for improvement in the seven examination categories. Overall, the written examinations provided a quite reliable picture of applicants, setting the stage for efficient and meaningful site visits.

Based upon the Judges' recommendations, Secretary Verity selected three Award winners for 1988. These are: Motorola Inc. and the Commercial Nuclear Fuel Division of Westinghouse Electric Corporation in the manufacturing category, and Globe Metallurgical, Inc. in the small business category. President Reagan presented the first Award at a ceremony in the White House on November 14, 1988.

In 1989, 40 companies applied for Awards: 23 in manufacturing, 6 in services, and 11 small businesses. Applications for 1989 are currently under review.

Feedback Reports

Feedback reports were sent to all applicants. The reports include general information on the evaluation process, scoring and overall results.

Specific feedback to applicants is primarily in the form of comments on strengths and areas for improvement in the seven categories that make up the examination. The reports also include statements of the scoring ranges reached by each of the applicants, along with the distribution of all scores.

Information Transfer

The information transfer strategy for 1988 and 1989 focused upon promoting awareness among key organizations which have a stake in quality improvement and which must participate if the national quality campaign is to succeed. Organizations contacted make up what might be called the quality "system" of the United States (Table 1).

Use of Award Criteria as an Information Transfer Device A major element in the national quality awareness campaign is to promote the use of the Award criteria in quality improvement. As of July 1989, approximately 40,000 copies of the 1989 Application Guidelines have been disseminated. In addition, other groups have duplicated copies and made them available in their companies or among their member organizations. Through contacts with application requestors, examiners, and others, a number of use patterns have been revealed (Table 2).

Organizations using the Award criteria include many which are currently ineligible to apply for Awards. Such organizations include business schools, community colleges, Federal agencies, nonprofit institutions, etc.

Activities of Award Winning Companies A major element in the information transfer strategy underlying the National Quality Award is built around the activities of the Award winning companies. Begin-

---

TABLE 1. QUALITY "SYSTEM" OF THE UNITED STATES

Professional and technical associations
Trade associations
Business groups
Area councils ("Communities of Excellence")
Universities and schools
State and local governments
Federal government
Accrediting bodies
Health care organizations

TABLE 2. USE OF THE MALCOLM BALDRIGE NATIONAL QUALITY AWARD CRITERIA

preparation for Awards—1990 and beyond
self assessment
training and education in companies
competition among divisions in companies
coordination among divisions in companies
companies working with suppliers and customers
trade associations promoting quality among members
business school education
basis for state awards
basis for local awards
general training courses
long-term goal setting

ning with the Award ceremony (November 14, 1988), the winning companies have conducted and participated in several hundred—information transfer activities—speaking, writing, hosting visitors, etc. In addition, they have held numerous celebrations and advertised in leading media in the U.S. The activities of the Award winners have proven to be the most significant generators of awareness. More importantly, perhaps, the winners have reinforced the definition of the parameters of world-class quality.

1. Curt W. Reimann, National Institute of Standards and Technology

INDEX